POLITENESS IN CHINESE FACE-TO-FACE INTERACTION

ADVANCES IN DISCOURSE PROCESSES

Roy O. Freedle, Series Editor

Vol. 1: *Discourse Production and Comprehension*
edited by Roy O. Freedle, 1977

Vol. 2: *New Directions in Discourse Processing*
edited by Roy O. Freedle, 1979

Vol. 3: *The Pear Stories: Cognitive, Cultural, and Linguistic Aspects of Narrative Production*
edited by Robert de Beaugrande, 1980

Vol. 4: *Text, Discourse, and Process: Toward a Multidisciplinary Science of Texts*
edited by Robert de Beaugrande, 1980

Vol. 5: *Ethnography and Language in Educational Settings*
edited by Judith Green and Cynthia Wallat, 1981

Vol. 6: *Latino Language and Communicative Behavior*
edited by Richard P. Duran, 1981

Vol. 7: *Narrative, Literacy, and Face in Interethnic Communication*
by Ron Scollon and Suzanne Scollon, 1981

Vol. 8: *Linguistics and the Professions*
edited by Robert J. DiPietro, 1982

Vol. 9: *Spoken and Written Language: Exploring Orality and Literacy*
edited by Deborah Tannen, 1982

Vol. 10: *Developmental Issues in Discourse*
edited by Jonathan Fine and Roy O. Freedle, 1983

Vol. 11: *Text Production: Toward a Science of Composition*
edited by Robert de Beaugrande, 1984

Printed in the United States of America

Library of Congress Cataloging-in-Publication Data

Pan, Yuling.
  Politeness in Chinese face-to-face interaction / by Yuling Pan.
      p.   cm. — (Advances in discourse processes v. 67)
      Includes bibliographical references and index.
      ISBN 1-56750-492-2—ISBN 1-56750-493-0 (pbk.)
      1. Etiquette—China.   2. Sociolinguistics—China.   3. China—Social
life and customs.   I. Title.   II. Series.
    BJ2007.C56 P34   2000
    302.3'4'0951—dc21   99-048931

Ablex Publishing Corporation
100 Prospect Street
P.O. Box 811
Stamford, CT 06904-0811

P

To my father, mother, and Wenzhi

Contents

ACKNOWLEDGMENTS

I would like to express my appreciation and gratitude to many people, colleagues, and friends who helped me during the various stages of this book. At its earliest stage, my professors at Georgetown University, Deborah Schiffrin, Deborah Tannen, and Roger Shuy, were continuing sources of intellectual guidance, support, and encouragement. I wish to thank all of them for introducing me to the field of sociolinguistics.

My debt to Ron Scollon and Suzanne Scollon goes further back than before I personally met them: their works on intercultural communication prompted me to develop most of the ideas here. Since January 1997, I have had the good fortune to work with them on various research projects in Hong Kong, Mainland China, Finland, and Washington, DC. They have provided most needed help and encouragement in various stages of this book, from the discussion of ideas to the reading of drafts. Their invaluable suggestions and insightful comments made this book complete. I thank them for their continuing patience, encouragement, and inspiration of my work.

My sincere thanks, also, to Patricia E. O'Connor and Barbara Craig, whose lasting support to me from the earliest stage until the very last phase of this book is a most valuable resource in this endeavor. They read the entire manuscript and gave me critical and useful comments. I also appreciate their help in editing the translations of the examples. I am grateful to Yoshiko Nakano, too, who read the earlier drafts, and has always been most supportive of my research and fieldwork.

I owe special thanks to my family and friends in China who assisted me in collecting data and who willingly became part of my data. They helped me get access to various organizations and institutions, and tape-recorded conversations and meetings for me. I am particularly grateful to my sister and my brother for patiently assisting me in the process of my research. Without their generous help, this project would not have been possible. Their contributions cannot be measured or described in words.

I also thank my research assistants and students at the City University of Hong Kong. I thank, in particular, Beatrice Chan, Cecilia Leung, Li Ming, Charlotte To, and Siu Ping Au for facilitating me in data preparation and double-checking the examples. Also my deep appreciation goes to Rachel Scollon for editing and proofreading the manuscript.

Special thanks also go to my American host family: Steven Kalish, Anita Bollt, Lauren Kalish, and Dana Kalish. The Kalish family was my first introduction to American culture, and they have been a continuing source of support for my work. I thank each of them.

My appreciation is also due to the City University of Hong Kong for several research grants that enabled me to go back to China for further investigation and data collection during my two years' work in Hong Kong. A Georgetown University Post-doctoral Fellowship allowed me a period of uninterrupted time to complete the final phase of this book. I thank these institutions for their financial and organizational assistance.

PREFACE

One important issue in intercultural communication is politeness phenomena across cultures. Too often I have encountered contradictory comments made by Americans about Chinese politeness practice. I began to research the topic as a subject of sociolinguistics, and later as a problem in intercultural communication. In this book, I describe Chinese politeness behavior across three social settings: business encounters, official meetings and family gatherings; and explain why Chinese seem to be inconsistent in their politeness behavior and why it is not easy to generalize about cultural characteristics. I also discuss how the sociological variables of power, distance, and imposition of an utterance function in different social settings, and the limitation of focusing our analysis of politeness on these variables only. I show that politeness behavior is a social practice that encodes the ideology and cultural values in a particular society, and that there are different assumptions about how to be polite in different cultures. In this study, linguistic politeness is examined not only at the syntactic or lexical level, but also at the level of discourse. I argue that discursive features contribute more to the signaling of politeness than the syntactic or lexical items in the Chinese language.

The body of the analysis is presented in chapters 2 through 5, using language data from naturally occurring face-to-face interactions collected through ethnographic research in Southern China. The three social settings of business encounters, official meetings, and family gatherings serve as the basis for my discussion on the significance of the distinction between inside and outside social relationships in the initial stage of social encounters, and the importance of acknowledging hierarchical structure in the inner circle while choosing face strategies. The last chapter discusses the characteristics of politeness practice in Chinese culture, and suggests an approach to understanding how and when face strategies are applied in social interactions.

I envision the analysis presented here having theoretical as well as practical applications. This book attempts to bring in the perspective of situational variation in analyzing linguistic politeness, and looks at politeness in the larger framework of social context. It outlines the way into the problem of politeness in Chinese culture and the steps taken in the application of politeness strategies in verbal interaction. This book has been written with the following audiences in mind:

1. Those who are interested in intercultural communication, and/or are interested in Chinese language and culture.
2. Professionals in various fields who deal with people from Chinese culture on a daily basis or on business trips, for example, foreign service personnel, government officials, business people, visiting scholars, and exchange students.
3. Students in introductory and graduate courses in intercultural communication, sociolinguistics, pragmatics, discourse analysis, and China studies.
4. Scholarly audiences in intercultural studies and discourse theory.

Data used as examples in this book are in two languages: Mandarin Chinese and Cantonese Chinese. For data in Mandarin Chinese, *pinyin*, the standard romanization system in the People's Republic of China is used to represent the original utterances. For data in Cantonese Chinese, the Cantonese Romanization Scheme established by the Linguistic Society of Hong Kong is adopted to transcribe the data. Arabic numerals are used to indicate the tone of each syllable (since both Mandarin and Cantonese Chinese are tonal languages), for example, *Zhong1guo2* (China).

Participants in this study are represented by pseudonyms. All Chinese names used in this book are pseudonyms, except for those of famous people. All translations from Chinese into English are my own.

What follows is my attempt to put together some ideas, observations, and experiences that answer the question of why Chinese have seemingly contradictory politeness behavior. This, of course, is only the beginning of the search for a better understanding of the problem.

1

INTRODUCTION: HOW POLITE ARE THE CHINESE?

China, being the world's most populous country, is taking a more and more active role in international affairs and global trade. Contacts with the Chinese in intercultural settings have become a challenge to people who are not familiar with Chinese culture. The Chinese have long been considered difficult to understand and deal with by Westerners, who perceive Chinese behavior as inscrutable and inconsistent. In this book I focus on one aspect of Chinese behavior, politeness practice, to reveal the complexities involved in communicating with the Chinese and a way into the understanding of Chinese politeness behavior.

To people who have lived in or been to China in recent years, the following two exchanges between a customer and a salesperson taking place in a Chinese store will sound quite familiar. In the first exchange, a female customer walks into the women's clothing section of a state-run department store and asks a saleswoman standing behind a counter to show her a sweater.

"

Example 1.1.   In a state-run department store

> 1. Customer: (pointing at the sweaters on display)
>   Give me that sweater to look at.

(The saleswoman takes down the sweater. The customer examines it)

> 2. Customer: Do you have a larger size?

(The saleswoman shakes her head)

> 3. Customer: (pointing at another sweater on display)
>   How about that one?

> 4. Saleswoman: That one is even smaller!
> 5. Customer: How much is this one?
> 6. Saleswoman: Ninety-eight dollars.

(The customer gives the saleswoman one hundred dollars. The saleswoman gives the change and the sweater to the customer)

This is typical of a service encounter in a state-run store in China, at least from the establishment of state-run business in the mid–1950s up to the early 1990s. In this kind of service encounter, the customer walks into the store and opens the interaction by making a direct request (for example, "Give me two stamps," "Show me that dress"). Often the customer has to yell for the salesclerk's attention. The salesclerk makes only a minimal verbal reply to the customer's request, gets out what the customer asks for, takes the money from the customer, and then gives the goods and change to the customer. During the whole interaction cited above, the saleswoman only speaks twice. Her first utterance in line 4 ("That one is even smaller") shows her impatience with the customer's request to look at another sweater, and the second one tells the customer the price (line 6). We can easily draw the conclusion that this interaction sounds very abrupt and gives the impression of being rude because: (1) there is no ritual opening and closing of the encounter, (2) there is no use of conventional politeness strategies, and (3) there is minimal verbal exchange between the customer and the clerk. The saleswoman uses body language (shaking the head) instead of verbal language in responding to the customer's request. This interaction runs counter to the popular belief in the West that Chinese are deferential and polite.

The second exchange takes place in a privately owned women's clothing shop. Again, a female customer walks in. This time, the saleswoman walks up to the customer and greets her.

Example 1.2.   In a privately owned store

1. Saleswoman: Hi, Mrs. Chen, I haven't seen you for a long time. Where have you been?
2. Customer: You know, I've been home with my new baby.
3. Saleswoman: What? You have a new baby!
4. Customer: Yes, I gave birth to a baby girl last August.
5. Saleswoman: Oh, but you look great. You're still so pretty and have a nice figure!
6. Customer: No, no, I've gained lots of weight.
7. Saleswoman: No, no, you're still in great shape! **What kind of clothing do you want to look at today?**
8. Customer: I'd like to see a dress.

(The saleswoman shows the customer a dress and the interaction goes on for some time)

This interaction has a completely different atmosphere from the first one and gives the feeling of friendly involvement between the saleswoman and the customer. In this interaction the saleswoman initiates the interaction by greeting the customer, who obviously has visited the store before. Then they both engage in a prolonged exchange about the customer's personal information (new baby) and an exchange of compliment-giving and declining before the saleswoman brings up the topic of the interaction ("What kind of clothing do you want to look at today?" line 7). The prolonged small talk between the server and the customer has created an effect of friendliness and involvement. By attending to personal issues and their relationship, the saleswoman has made the customer feel good and welcomed, of course with the ultimate goal of selling her something.

Westerners who experienced an interaction such as that in Example 1.1 might conclude that Chinese are quite rude and cold, while those who encountered the second interaction would conclude that Chinese are very friendly and polite but pry too much into personal life. It is true that there are polite and impolite practices in any culture, and that people of any cultural group can be nice or rude. But these two contradictory cases raise some questions: Why do people of the same culture differ a great deal in their politeness behavior on two seemingly similar occasions? What makes them different if there is any difference? And how can we account for politeness behavior in a particular culture?

There are two issues of politeness study that I want to address in this book. One is the problems that arise when people try to look for what Chinese politeness is amid the general pattern in cultural differences among, say, Chinese, Americans, Japanese, or Germans. The first problem is that we tend to draw a conclusion about cultural difference and attribute problems to cultural differences when we examine politeness behavior of a cultural group in general cultural terms without looking into the subtle sociocultural variables governing the interaction in a specific situation. It is true that there are cultural differences between people from different cultural backgrounds, but culture may not be the sole explanation for the difference. In the above two cases, the participants are of the same cultural background, but behave differently in the two very similar encounters. If we lump Chinese politeness behavior together, it is easy for us to fall into a binary comparison of cultural differences and develop either a positive or a negative stereotype. For instance, during my 10 years' teaching of Chinese language and culture to U.S. foreign service officers in the United States, I often heard contradictory remarks about Chinese made by my students who had worked and lived in China. One of them said: "Chinese are very polite." When asked why, the student said: "They treat their guests like kings, so hospitable, so warm." Another student commented: "Chinese are so rude." When asked for an explanation, he said: "When you go to a store to buy things, the shop attendants are very rude. They throw the change at you and don't say a word." They often commented on whether Chinese are polite or rude, but rarely mentioned the situation. Only when asked for an explanation did they recollect the situation. Their recollection of Chinese politeness shows the common practice of looking at politeness behavior without putting it into context and without making a distinction between situations. The question is not whether Chinese are polite or not, but what the dominant practice is in a specific situation and what politeness strategies are called for in that particular situation. This leads to the second problem that I would like to address in this book.

The second issue is what should be included in our study of politeness behavior. This encompasses the basic question of how to examine politeness behavior and how to determine politeness strategies in face-to-face interaction. Previous politeness studies (for example, Brown & Levinson, 1987; Scollon & Scollon, 1995) propose the sociological variables of relative power and social distance between the participants and the imposition of a face-threatening act (Brown & Levinson's term, 1987). In the above two cases, we have more or less the same sociological variables. There is a similar power structure due to the same social relationship between the participants, seller and potential buyer. It is the same speech situation, a service encounter involving buying clothes. But if we look further into the relational and organizational dimensions, we shall see that there are two differences between the two cases. One is the interpersonal relationship between the customer and the salesclerk (unacquainted versus acquainted). The second is the organizational structure of the two stores (state-run versus privately owned). The first difference can be accounted for as the variable of social distance. But how to account for the second difference? Should we go into such detailed contextual analysis when examining linguistic politeness? How about other situational factors such as the type of setting, social attributes of the addressee, and source of power? What role do they play in our determination of politeness strategies? What are the social practices associated with politeness behavior in different situations? These are the issues that I shall discuss in the following chapters.

WHY POLITENESS?

Politeness is part of our world knowledge about how to behave appropriately in a given situation and how to maintain smooth interactions and good social relationships with other people. It involves human psychological needs, psychological and social identity, and interpersonal and social relationships. In face-to-face interaction, linguistic politeness, that is, the use of language to attend to each other's face needs, helps to mitigate utterances that may otherwise impose a threat to other people's face. In other words, linguistic politeness has the function of reducing the risk of hurting other people's feelings when we have to say something that we think may be abrupt or rude. It also amplifies the effect of making others feel good when we want to say something nice.

Politeness is also one of the crucial issues in cross-cultural and intercultural studies. When we go to a new place, a new culture, and meet new people, one of the first things that we want to know is how to be polite, how to act appropriately, and how to avoid offending people, because we do not want to get into trouble by innocently violating the rules of other cultures, including the politeness rules. Various cross-cultural studies compare and contrast politeness behavior of different cultural groups, and it has become one of the important topics in intercultural training for diplomatic personnel, multinational corporations, and business people. Not only is politeness an important aspect of our ability to get along with people in a new cultural environment, but quite often our first impression of a cultural group is based on whether we think people from that culture are nice and polite or not. Our judgment of other people is based on our own concept of what is good and what is bad, what is considered to be polite and what is considered impolite. It is quite tempting for us, in order to know what to expect, to draw the line of what IS and what is NOT polite based on our own value system, which may or may not hold true in another culture.

Most often we find it simplest to learn a set of rules for how to behave in a new culture and tend to judge if people are polite or impolite. But many times we are not aware that our perception of politeness is part of our discourse system, which consists of ideology, socialization, face system, and form of discourse (Scollon & Scollon, 1995). Our idea of how to be polite is the product of our socialization. If people do not share the same discourse system in any particular situation, their perceptions of politeness and power relations will not be identical. Much misunderstanding or miscommunication occurring in cross-cultural settings is the result of the misreading of involvement and independence, the imbalance of power and rapport (Tannen, 1986, 1990), and misjudgment of others' intentions. That is because the practice of politeness is not just a set of fixed rules, but rather it is a set of deep-rooted cultural beliefs concerning the perception of power relations, concept of self and other, and understanding of interpersonal relationships. Each individual, in his/her early socialization process, learns these concepts while acquiring interpersonal skills and cultural tools to deal with different situations. Thus, to understand the politeness behavior of a cultural group requires understanding the ideologies governing social practices in that culture and the cultural values embedded in linguistic politeness.

For example, anthropologist Francis Hsu (1981) has described differing configurations of self for Americans and Chinese. Mapping the self in layers of concentric circles, he says that Americans draw a boundary between the individual's expressive conscious and his or her intimate associates, while Chinese include intimate associates within the boundary of the self. This means that for Americans the individual is the basic unit of self, while for Chinese self is larger in that it includes not only the individual, but also intimate family members. What this implies is that the individual's concern for face is more important for the relational nuclei where the individual is paramount than where group boundaries are relatively permanent. Politeness strategies in American culture would thus tend to address the individual's face needs, while in Chinese culture politeness strategies would attend to the relational and hierarchical dimensions.

Some of the questions most often asked by my U.S. foreign service students are "How can I behave appropriately in Chinese culture?" "What are the rules for being polite in China?" "What can I do to avoid hurting Chinese people's face?" At first I tried to give them rule-of-thumb guidelines, such as that Chinese are very concerned about face, very deferential to their superiors, and like to talk about personal issues. I later realized this sometimes creates more trouble than it averts, because when people try to deal with cultural differences, they sometimes actually make matters worse in their attempts at cultural sensitivity (Scollon & Scollon, 1995). Many times the rule-of-thumb guideline does not provide an explanation for cultural values and situational variations. One Finnish diplomat stationed in Beijing gave an interesting account of how Finnish companies train their employees to be sensitive to Chinese concepts of face and connection (*guanxi*) when doing business in China. The employees became so much afraid of upsetting Chinese counterparts' face that before every sentence they had to stop and think whether it would be face-threatening, to the point of not knowing how to talk to Chinese. But as we have seen in cases such as the example in the state-run store, there is absolutely no facework performed. The Finns face-saving stalemates then would be counter to actual practice. Yet this runs counter to the general belief that face concern is paramount in Chinese culture. The question that remains is why there is such a gap between the general belief and the reality.

When I first started researching Chinese politeness behavior, I was tempted to take the cultural approach to find out whether Chinese are polite or not by using a set of established politeness strategies. I found myself caught in the dilemmas of determining what criteria should be applied and of determining how to make the judgment. I also found that it is hard to draw a clear-cut distinction between a face-saving utterance and one that serves some other function without looking into contextual elements. It is equally difficult to say what Chinese politeness is like without knowing the situation. Just as in the cases cited by foreign service officers at the beginning of this chapter, Chinese seem to be very rude on one occasion and very polite on another. The point is, if we do not take into account the situation in which an interaction takes place, it is quite superficial to examine whether an act is polite or not. This is because: (1) face-to-face interaction is an on-going negotiation process (Gumperz, 1982), and participants constantly adjust their face strategies to suit each other's needs; and (2) power relations which are considered to be the main parameter in deciding the choice of politeness strategies, change from setting to setting. This is a dynamic relationship rather than a static one. A speaker's power comes from various sources: rank, age, gender, expertise, money, knowledge, and so forth. Which source of power is the deciding one in our determination of politeness strategies depends on the situation.

A scene from the Chinese classic *The Dream of the Red Mansion* (Cao, 1791) provides a typical example. The emperor's concubine, accompanied by imperial officials, comes to visit her own family for the first time since becoming the emperor's concubine. When she arrives at her father's house, the whole family receives her with formal rituals in the family hall. The father, a high ranking official in the royal palace, kneels before her and kowtows. Since this is a formal occasion, and because of her association with the emperor, the daughter is higher in the official hierarchy than her father. He observes the formal rituals appropriate to an official setting. Afterwards, the state officials leave the scene and the welcoming ceremony is over. The family gathers in the family room. This time, the concubine kneels down and kowtows to her father because it is now a father-daughter scenario. This example shows how the change of setting changes power relations and participants' sensitivity to the different roles they play in different situations. Politeness rituals are predetermined by situational conditions.

My purpose in this book, then, is to disclose the complexity of the sources of power that govern Chinese politeness behavior in different settings. I will argue for a situation-specific approach to politeness phenomena by examining, face-to-face interactions in three settings: service encounters, official meetings, and family gatherings. These are common situations that most of us encounter in our day-to-day life. The illustration of how the dynamics of social relations and power structures are interwoven in politeness phenomena in these situations will help us understand the complexity of politeness behavior patterns in Chinese culture.

APPROACHES TO POLITENESS

There are two main approaches to the study of politeness: language-based and society-based. The language-based approach treats politeness as part of pragmatic knowledge and as the linguistic realizations of pragmatic rules in communication. Lakoff's (1973, 1974) politeness rules and Leech's (1983) politeness principles are typical of this approach. Common to these theories is the assumption of rationality in human behavior. Both Lakoff and Leech deal with politeness as a complementary element to Gricean Maxims of Cooperation (Grice, 1975). The basic assumption is that human behaviors, though seemingly random, are rule-governed and that just as there are grammatical rules governing our linguistic structure, there are rules relating to the pragmatic aspect of language use. We follow pragmatic rules in speaking, just as we follow semantic and syntactic rules, and all must be a part of our linguistic knowledge. There are two basic pragmatic rules that speakers follow in communication: (1) be clear; (2) be polite (Lakoff, 1979). The first, "be clear," is in observation of Gricean maxims in conversation while "be polite" is in service of the higher goal in communication—to fulfill the social function of language. This explains why speakers regularly and intentionally refrain from saying what they mean. These two basic rules of pragmatics sometimes coincide in their effect. Depending on the circumstances, one or the other will supersede, but they reinforce each other more often than they are in conflict. If one seeks to communicate a message directly, he/she will attempt to be clear; if the speaker's aim is to navigate among the respective statuses of the participants, he/she will aim at an expression of politeness. When clarity conflicts with politeness, in most cases politeness supersedes.

Lakoff develops three rules of politeness (later called Rules of Rapport): (1) don't impose; (2) give options; and (3) be friendly. Following each of these rules creates a certain stylistic effect in communication. The rule of "don't impose" gives the feeling of being distant. The rule of "give options" shows deference to the hearer, and the rule of "be friendly" creates camaraderie between the speaker and the hearer. These stylistic effects are associated with politeness notions, indicating the relationship between the interlocutors in relation to the situation. These politeness strategies are not ordered hierarchically but rather as points on a continuum, with Gricean maxims at one end and camaraderie at the other. The use of rules depends on the situation and purpose: whether to exchange information or to seek social relationship. If efficient information exchange is the purpose, then the rule of clarity (Gricean maxims) is applied. When rapport is being sought, rules of politeness are followed.

Leech also treats politeness as that part of pragmatics that helps to explain why what is said is not always equivalent to what is meant. For him, politeness provides a missing link between the Gricean Cooperative Principle (CP) and the problem of how to relate sense to the effect of a speech act (force). In Leech's model, rationality is the key. The Cooperative Principle and Politeness Principle are observed because human interaction is goal-directed and human agents recognize that their interactional goals can only be obtained if they cooperate with each other. Politeness is constructed out of the Politeness Principle made up of six maxims, namely: the tact, generosity, approbation, modesty, agreement, and sympathy maxims. But not all of the maxims are equally important. Certain maxims are stressed in some cultures and not in others.

Leech makes a distinction between relative politeness and absolute politeness. Relative politeness refers to the fact that politeness is often relative to context or situation, whereas absolute politeness is seen as a scale or rather set of scales having a negative and a positive pole. At the negative end of the pole is negative politeness consisting of minimizing the impoliteness of impolite illocutions (for example, an order). At the positive end is positive politeness consisting of maximizing the politeness of polite illocutions (for example, an invitation). In his model, Leech emphasizes the normative aspect of politeness and primarily deals with absolute politeness.

The politeness rules and principles proposed by Lakoff and Leech answer the philosophical questions of why people do not always say what they mean and how people can be seen as being cooperative without following the Cooperative Principle. These rules can be considered as the basis for politeness phenomena in human interaction. But just as Leech claims, these rules account for absolute politeness, that is, politeness out of social context. Since human communication is always situated in some kind of context, we need to know when and under what conditions we can apply certain rules in dealing with people in communication. This book is my attempt to look at the relative side of politeness. I feel that absolute politeness is like linguistic competence, *la langue,* while relative politeness is like language performance, *la parole.* It is relative politeness that is exhibited in our actual communication and that causes misunderstanding or problems in intercultural or cross-cultural communication. What we express in politeness is not just our good will to attend to social relationships, but also our perception of power. The perception of power differs in its cultural and contextual terms. When a person follows the "be friendly" rule in a home environment or with friends, he/she assumes an equal power dimension. But in an official context, a superior following the rule of "be friendly" to a subordinate entails a power disparity because the subordinate can not reciprocate the strategy. The superior has the option either to show rapport by "being friendly" or to show power, but the subordinate does not have that option. The subordinate is usually expected to follow the rule of deference and in most cases will do so (Tannen, 1994; Pan, 1994). In other words, the use of these politeness rules may not always produce the same effect in different settings. Therefore, it is important to take situational and contextual variations into account in investigating politeness behavior.

Another widely cited theory arising out of the language-based approach to politeness is Brown and Levinson's politeness model (1987). Although Brown and Levinson discuss sociological variables in politeness phenomena, their focus is still the linguistic realization of that part of pragmatic rules called politeness. Central to Brown and Levinson's model is the concept of face, which is much discussed in the study of interpersonal relationships by anthropologists and sociologists (for example, Goffman, 1959, 1967; Ho, 1976; Hu, 1944). It has the social and psychological implication of honor, public image, positive social value, or social prestige claimed for oneself. In Brown and Levinson's influential politeness model, face is treated as the universal human psychological need, and it is assumed that a rational human being possesses two aspects of face: positive face and negative face. Positive face is "the positive consistent self-image or 'personality' (crucially including the desire that this self-image be appreciated and approved of) claimed by interactants" (Brown & Levinson, 1987, p. 61). Negative face is "the basic claim to territories, personal preserves, rights to non-distraction—i.e., to freedom of action and freedom from imposition" (Brown & Levinson, 1987, p. 61). Positive face and negative face represent the two paradoxical needs of human beings: the need to be liked and be part of a group, and the need to be respected and be independent. During face-to-face interaction, these face needs are vulnerable to face-threatening acts encoded in language (abbreviated hereafter as FTAs), which either threaten the involvement aspect of the relationship between the participants or impede the independence of individuals. For example, a request makes an imposition on the hearer to carry out a certain action. This hinders the hearer's autonomy of action, that is, negative face need. If the request is phrased in such a way that it sounds very polite and distant, it might impede the hearer's wish to be helpful and be involved, that is, positive face need. Therefore linguistic politeness strategies are employed to reduce the imposition of FTAs so that the participants' positive and negative face needs can be addressed during the interaction. So politeness is a face-saving device, functioning to preserve face so that human interaction can proceed smoothly.

Brown and Levinson list three sociological variables that affect our use of politeness strategies: (1) the relative power (P) between the speaker and hearer; (2) the relative social distance (D) between the speaker and hearer; and (3) the ranking (R) of imposition of FTAs. Depending on the amount of concern for face and the calculation of these three variables, P, D and R, speakers determine which of the following face strategies they will use: (1) bald on-record—the direct way of saying things; (2) positive politeness—the expression of solidarity; (3) negative politeness—the expression of restraint; (4) off-record politeness—the avoidance of unequivocal impositions, for example, hints; and (5) don't do FTAs. Brown and Levinson's contribution to the study of politeness is the distinction of the two aspects of face (positive face and negative face) and the linguistic strategies that attend to these two face wants. This distinction reflects the paradox of human beings' psychological needs of involvement and independence in language use. Individuals need to be connected with others while at the same time remain relatively independent. Both bald-on-record and positive politeness strategies address our need to be connected with other social members while negative politeness and off-record strategies satisfy our need to be free of imposition from others. The starting point of Brown and Levinson's model is also a rational individual free of sociocultural and contextual influence.

Their model has evoked numerous studies by researchers in sociolinguistics and cross-cultural studies. Their original theory and the concept of face were examined and extended in different cultural contexts. Three major issues were raised concerning their model: (1) the universality of the notion of face; (2) the weighting of the sociological variables of power, distance, and imposition in different cultures; and (3) whether an FTA is really face-threatening in all cultures.

The most controversial issue is the universals of the notion of face and the treatment of face: whether face should be treated as an independent phenomenon or an interdependent phenomenon. Scholars studying Asian politeness (for example, Chang & Holt, 1994; Gu, 1990; Ide, 1982, 1989; Mao, 1994; Matsumoto, 1988, 1989; Morisaki & Gudykunst, 1994) question the conceptualization and universality of face in Brown and Levinson's politeness theory. They maintain that Brown and Levinson's treatment of face as an independent phenomenon is based on the western cultural value of individualism while face is an interdependent phenomenon in Asian societies in which collectivism is the dominant cultural value. Therefore, some scholars (for example, Ting-Toomey, 1988) argue for a distinction between individualistic and collectivistic cultures in terms of the sense of self and the concept of face. In individualistic cultures like that of North America, self is independent of others and face is an individual's public image. In collectivistic cultures like those of China and Japan, on the other hand, self is a more inclusive concept, and interdependent with others. Face is then an inter-relational concern. Due to the difference in face concepts, motivation for the use of politeness strategies is not the same in these two types of culture. For example, negative politeness is motivated by the respect for the other's independence and autonomy of action in an individualistic culture, but is required by the social norm of respecting hierarchical order in a collectivistic society. Therefore, it is crucial to take into account sociocultural elements in the consideration of face and politeness.

The second issue of the weighing of power, distance, and imposition raises two questions: Are these variables of equal importance in all cultures? How can we account for FTAs in different languages? For instance, what constitutes power may differ from culture to culture. It may be age, gender, rank, economic status, political position, professional field, social class, educational background, or family ties depending on cultural values. In the same light, the measurement of social distance also shows cultural differences. For Americans, a five-minute conversation between two strangers can close the social distance and the participants could then be on a first-name basis in talking to each other (Fasold, 1990). But for Chinese the social distance is so immense that it is extremely difficult to cross group boundaries. It is also a life-time obligation to maintain the hierarchical relationship between group members.

The third issue of how to account for an FTA also pertains to cultural values. A speech act that is assumed to be imposing in one culture may not have the same effect in another culture. In Japanese culture, a request from a subordinate to a superior asking the superior to take care of him/her is not considered face-threatening. Rather it enhances the face of the superior by recognizing the hierarchical difference between the participants (Matsumoto, 1988). In Chinese culture, a direct suggestion is considered a display of good will instead of making an imposition on the hearer (Pan, 1994). So whether an FTA is really face-threatening depends upon the type of relationship, situation, and the cultural values attached to the relationship and situation. Many studies have investigated conditions for speech acts in different languages with the aim of discovering cultural norms and politeness rules for performing speech acts in different cultures. This type of study mainly focuses on single speech acts and contributes to the language-based approach to politeness.

The society-based approach to politeness is best represented by Scollon and Scollon's (1995) politeness system. While other studies of politeness strategies focus on a single type of speech act such as requests, compliments, invitations, or apologies, Scollon and Scollon extend the study of politeness to another level of communication: discourse. They aim to discover the whole communicative system of which a politeness system is a part. Based upon Brown and Levinson's model, Scollon and Scollon outline the characteristics of three types of politeness systems, solidarity politeness system, deference politeness system, and hierarchical politeness system, and possible conflicts resulting from differences among these three types of systems. In their treatment of politeness, relative power and social distance are still the main sociological variables that determine the use of two politeness strategies: involvement and independence strategies. (These two terms were introduced by Tannen (1986) and are used in Scollon and Scollon's politeness systems to avoid the negative association of Brown and Levinson's terms of positive and negative politeness.) But they emphasize that a politeness system is part of a discourse system which consists of ideology, socialization, forms of discourse, and face systems. The element of ideology and process of socialization determine the preferred human relationships and face systems in a specific society.

The three main types of politeness systems are based primarily on the power difference (+P or −P) and the distance between participants (+D or −D). In a deference politeness system, participants are considered to be equal in power relations and treat each other at a distance using independence strategies which correspond to what Brown and Levinson call "negative politeness." This kind of system favors deference, indirectness, or even avoidance of making impositions on others at all. In this type of system the differences among members are emphasized. The assumption is that one may not easily anticipate the needs or wants of others and any impositions are made in the context of careful respect for the rights of the other. In a solidarity politeness system, participants see themselves as equal in social position and in a close social relation. They both use politeness strategies of involvement which correspond to Brown and Levinson's positive politeness. The solidarity politeness system emphasizes sameness or commonality of group membership, and the general good of the group. The strategies most often employed are bald-on-record and positive politeness. The third kind of politeness system is the hierarchical politeness system. In this type of system the participants recognize and respect the social differences that place one in a superordinate position and the other in a subordinate position (Scollon & Scollon, 1995, p. 45). The relationships are asymmetrical in that the participants do not use the same face politeness strategies in speaking to each other. The person in the superordinate position speaks "down" by using involvement strategies (which correspond to positive politeness). The person in the subordinate position speaks "up" using independence strategies (which correspond to negative politeness).

Scollon and Scollon's treatment of politeness phenomena outlines the complexity of the interaction of relative power, social distance, face strategies and cultural values in interpersonal communication. A significant application of their study is in intercultural communication. When people with different communicative systems come into contact, communication problems are not caused by grammar or lexicon so much as by differences in discourse systems, politeness systems, and sociocultural conditions that predetermine the speaker's role and communication patterns. If the hierarchical politeness system is the preferred practice in one culture, for example, in Chinese and Korean culture, people from the solidarity politeness system would be perceived as crossing the line and even being rude when they use involvement strategies toward a person in a superordinate position. Similarly, when the solidarity politeness system is the expected norm in a situation, the use of independence strategies can be perceived as aloof and cold.

Scollon and Scollon (1991, 1994) point out distinctive features of Asian discourse phenomena (for example, topic introduction, turn-taking) and face concern in inside (*nei*) and outside (*wai*) relationships. Inside and outside relationships constitute situational dependency of face wants as suggested by Tracy (1990), who has also argued that studies of face must take into consideration that "the face wants (that is, identity claims) to which people orient are dependent on situation, personality, and culture" (p. 218). Inside relationships are the five classical Confucian relationships (ruler-ruled, father-son, husband-wife, elder-younger, friend-friend) as well as a host of "*tong*" (same) relationships (same school, same town, same employer). Outside relationships are occasional and temporary relationships with strangers that a person happens to come into contact with, such as shop clerks, bank tellers, or taxi drivers. Within the inside relationships, the hierarchical relationship between two speakers decides who speaks first and what face strategies should be used by each participant. This concept has great explanatory power with regard to Chinese politeness behavior, answering the question of why Chinese seem inscrutable and clarifying some of the perceived contradictions in Chinese behavior. The two cases cited at the beginning of this chapter display some of the differences in how people behave in outside and inside relationships. The encounter taking place in the state-run store between the female customer and the salesclerk is treated as an interaction between people in an outside relationship because it is perceived as a temporary encounter and the customer and the clerk are not likely to meet again. Thus no facework is called for. In contrast, the interaction between Mrs. Chen and the saleswoman in the private store is treated as an inside one, though they are not closely connected. As Mrs. Chen is an old customer of the store and the saleswoman knows her, the relationship is already established as one of acquaintanceship. There is a kind of business connection between the two. The saleswoman is trying to build on this connection by attending to the positive face—the need to be liked—of the customer through extended facework, such as greeting her and complimenting her on her good figure. Thus, the distinction between inside and outside relationships determines the way people interact with each other and the type of face strategies used in their interaction.

SITUATION-BASED APPROACH TO POLITENESS

Both language-based and society-based approaches provide significant insights into the understanding of politeness. Following the language-based approach, researchers in cross-cultural studies compare and contrast linguistic strategies that attend to face need in a variety of languages. The main focus for many of these studies is on syntactic structures and lexical items that signal politeness in a particular language or that show how a speech act is performed with face redressive strategies in a specific culture. Central to the language-based approach is the notion of a context-free rational human being following politeness rules in communication. Thus, the situational difference is not treated as a variable in this school of thoughts. The findings from these studies often tend to suggest generalizations about the behavior patterns of a cultural group, such as that Americans are direct, Japanese are indirect, and Chinese are very concerned about face. While this type of general principle can be a highly valuable resource for cross-cultural understanding, we must take the analysis a step further to fully understand politeness phenomena in a specific culture. Let us go back to the two cases of service encounters at the beginning of this chapter. In the state-run store, neither the customer nor the shop clerk shows any face concern for each other. The interaction is very direct and task-oriented. In the privately owned store, however, both the customer and the saleswoman engage in some kind of facework before they get down to business. On the basis of these examples we cannot say that Chinese are very concerned with face. Nor can we say Chinese are not concerned with face. What triggers the difference in politeness behavior in two similar interactions in this homogeneous culture?

The essence of politeness is dealing appropriately with others in a given communicative situation. If contextual elements are left out of the analysis, the comparison is only at the level of linguistic structure and leaves much cultural difference unaccounted for. In fact, the concept of politeness exists in any culture, and linguistic politeness strategies exist in any language. The cultural difference lies not so much in how politeness is realized linguistically, but in preference for a certain type of politeness strategy in a specific situation and in interpretation of the five basic elements in face-to-face interaction: face, setting, goal, role relationship, and power relations. The interpretation of these elements determines our choice of linguistic politeness strategies. For instance, if face is interpreted as an independent aspect in a cultural group, then independence strategies are the preferred way of expressing politeness in that culture. If face is treated as an interdependent concern in a culture, involvement strategies should be more common. But this is not absolute, because the setting and the goal of an interaction intersect with face concern and act together to determine the role relationship and power structure.

Scollon and Scollon's society-based approach outlines the cultural conditions for the use of different politeness strategies. At the core of their politeness systems is the perception of power relationships in communication in different settings. The problem that remains, though, is determining what is counted as the most important source of power in a specific situation. Again, the three politeness systems of deference, solidarity, and hierarchy exist in all cultures. What is more important is our perception of what power relationship we are in when we deal with others and which politeness system is the preferred practice in a specific situation. I believe it is at this level that we can expound on cultural differences. Cultural differences arise not only in our reaction to power relations, but in our interpretation of situational differences as well. For instance, do we give paramount attention to individuals or to hierarchical structure? If hierarchical structure is the basic system in human relationships in a society, then it is not perceived as appropriate to claim equal position or status by using involvement strategies with a person in a superordinate position. Our perception of the source of power in a specific situation, whether it comes from age, gender, rank, money, race, or the like, also reveals cultural differences. As I will show in the following chapters, it is true that Chinese are sensitive to the hierarchical order between speakers, and linguistic politeness signals this concern. But the power that decides a speaker's position in the hierarchical structure comes from different sources in different settings. The most important thing is to pinpoint the source of power in a specific situation and the politeness strategies employed to show that power relation and face need.

In this respect, ethnography of communication offers insight into face-to-face interaction and shows how politeness plays a part in our dealings with others. Ethnography of communication as defined by Hymes (1962, 1972, 1974), Saville-Troike (1989), and others emphasizes the importance of the contextual elements of situation, setting, relationship between participants, and goal of an interaction when analyzing language use. This theory lays out the basic structure of human communication. In other words, communication does not take place in a vacuum. Contextual elements are as important as the language code itself in successful communication. Changes in one of these contextual elements can lead to different interpretations of the language code. A conversation with a salesclerk in a shop may be interpreted quite differently from one held in a family gathering in terms of its purpose and goal. In fact, identification of the situation and type of relationship is the first step people take in communication. Scollon (1998) sets out maxims of stance in face-to-face interaction with a nested set of social practices such that primary real-time attention is given to the establishment of the frame of the event, called the channel. After the channel is established, attention is given to the relationship and identity. When identities have been established, attention is given to topic. Put another way, in opening a conversation or a discourse, participants first define the situation or frame the event of the interaction. Is it a personal telephone call between friends or a business call from your boss? Is it a business lunch or a social gathering with colleagues? When the situation has been defined, participants attend to the positioning of their relationship. Who is high and who is low in the hierarchical structure? What is the distance between the two participants? After that, participants attend to the topics of the interaction. What is the communicative focus of the situation? What is the topic about? Scollon suggests that of the three levels of social practice, the broadest level of situation is fundamental for an analysis of face-to-face communication.

This applies to the analysis of politeness phenomena as well. The sociological variables of power, distance, and weight of imposition in the determination of face strategies vary with situations. Definition of the situation or framing of the event is the initial step we take in determining how to act appropriately or politely. Therefore I propose a situation-based approach to politeness phenomena through looking at social relationship (inside versus outside), power relationship (the source of power), speakers' social attributes (rank, age, gender), and variation of politeness behavior across situations. The question here is not whether these factors exist in a particular culture, but the degree to which these factors affect our behavior and the relative importance of each factor in determining power relations. In other words, cultural differences may be found in the extent to which people pay attention to the distinction between inside and outside relationship in social interaction, to the source of power, and to the nature of the situation in their use of politeness strategies. In this model, culture cannot be the only explanation of Chinese or any culture's politeness behavior. Differences in behavior arise not only because of cultural variation, but also from situational variation. The two examples at the beginning of this chapter demonstrate that even within a homogeneous culture people's behavior can be very different. An explanatory approach focusing on culture alone is too simplistic a view to account for the complexity of human behavior, and is more likely to develop a barrier in intercultural communication than to bridge the gap. The situation-based approach, then, allows internal diversity within a culture, treating culture as being distributive rather than being uniform and stable (cf. Rodseth, 1998).

Recently I had an interesting encounter with a group of Finns working in Beijing. One of my colleagues was giving a talk on intercultural communication to a group of expatriates in Beijing. During a casual conversation before the talk, a Finnish man told a joke about the reticent Finns. Everybody laughed at his joke and agreed that the Finns are a very silent people. Then during my colleague's talk, a Finnish woman sitting next to me was talking all the time to the woman next to her. She talked so much that other people in the audience kept turning around, trying to silence her. After my colleague's talk, she went up to him and said, "What you said about the Finns is very true. We Finns are very quiet people. I only talk in a professional setting. I don't speak like this when I'm at home." This Finnish woman's behavior is opposite the common belief that Finns are reticent and silent (cf. "The Silent Finn" by Lehtonen & Sajavaara, 1985; "The Silent Finn Revisited" by Sajavaara & Lehtonen, 1997). She made the point that she acts differently in different settings. People take up different social roles and appropriate cultural tools from different sources to act according to the situation. This woman was trained as an interpreter and was at that time working as a diplomat; she may have appropriated her working communication style from her professional training. It is indeed inadequate to describe the behavior pattern of a culture group without looking into variation across settings. This example also shows that people are aware that they may use different strategies in different settings. People pay close attention to situational variations, maybe subconsciously, shift their identities, and use the appropriate strategies in different settings. What sociolinguists can do is to uncover the characteristics of situational factors and bring them to the conscious level of communicators. This is the first goal of this study.

My second goal is to examine politeness at the discursive level. Politeness strategies are not necessarily confined to the level of syntax and lexicon. Indeed, discourse strategies—including opening/closing, topic introduction, turn-taking, response, and conflict management—are as closely related to face concerns as are certain syntactic structures and lexical items that serve as politeness hedges. Scollon and Scollon's research on Asian discourse has demonstrated the close relationship between face concern and topic introduction. Tannen's (1986, 1990) works on conversational style have shown how involvement and independence are interpreted through such discourse elements as topic control, turn-taking, question-answer, and pausing. Including these discourse elements in the discussion of politeness strategies will broaden our understanding of politeness phenomena. Thus in my analysis of politeness strategies, I take the whole interaction as the basic unit and look for strategies that attend to face concerns at the discursive as well as syntactic level. I find that politeness in Chinese is expressed much more through discursive strategies than lexical items in face-to-face interaction. I shall discuss this in detail in the following chapters.

VARIATION ACROSS SETTINGS: THREE SETTINGS

Most of the current studies on Chinese politeness either deal with only one type of situation—such as conversation among friends or families, or between teachers and students (Gu, 1990; Lii Shih, 1986, 1994; Mao, 1994), or use literature as the source of data (Zhan, 1992). While these studies explicate the basic practice of Chinese politeness behavior, the crucial issue of how situation determines interaction remains untouched. The importance of sociocultural conditions to politeness behavior in Chinese society is the point I intend to convey in this book. I shall examine Chinese politeness in a broad way, taking into account the social factors of age, gender, rank, ingroup identity, and setting. Chinese anthropologist Francis Hsu (1981) characterizes Chinese behavior as being situation-centered, in contrast to individual-centered American behavior. That is, Chinese tend to care more about what one is expected to do under certain circumstances rather than what one wants to do. The emphasis is placed upon "an individual's appropriate place and behavior among his fellowmen" (1981, p. 12) and therefore, a Chinese is "inclined to be socially or psychologically dependent on others, for this situation-centered individual is tied closer to his world and his fellowmen" (1981, p. 13). For this reason, Chinese are more concerned with external factors such as how others think about "me" than the internal factor of what "I" think. Everybody wants to make sure that he/she is doing the right thing in relation to everybody else. As a result, the underlying force for Chinese politeness is acknowledgment of situational factors incorporated in the setting.

To further elaborate the significance of the distinction between inside and outside relationships in Chinese politeness behavior, I chose to investigate Chinese politeness behavior in three settings that represent a variety of situations and power structures: service encounters, professional meetings, and family gatherings. I shall illustrate how Chinese people in various relationships—superior-subordinate, colleague-colleague, service person–customer, friend-friend, and family member–family member—interact with each other and act out the social roles and relationships that are coupled with situations. I will also examine what constitutes power in a specific situation, how participants respond to that source of power, and what cultural tools they appropriate to cope with the situation.

An official setting represents the most formal aspect of social life. China is a society that places great importance on social hierarchy. Government officials have always enjoyed the highest social status of all the social classes. The traditional social order recognized four major social classes. In order of declining importance these were officials, peasants, handicraftsmen, and businessmen. Within the official system, one's rank decides his (or, rarely, her) place in the hierarchy, and thus power is closely tied to rank. Naturally, the rank hierarchy is emphasized in an official setting and people are aware of the importance of maintaining this hierarchy. Very often, participants need to have an idea of each other's social attributes in order to behave appropriately within this hierarchical structure. Attention is paid to how to use politeness strategies to signal social differences appropriately.

In this book, official setting is used to refer to formal occasions such as business meetings in government organizations as well as in companies. In China up until the early 1990s, all organizations were government organizations and all businesses were state-run except for some small-scale cooperative businesses in rural areas. Employees in all walks of life were government employees, including those working in the business sector, educational and medical field, manufacturing as well as service industries. The economic reform started in the early 1980s changed this structure to some extent. Currently there is a mixed state of economy, and there are state-run as well as private businesses in China. Government employees are ranked according to the official ranking system created after the 1949 Revolution in an effort to diminish social classes. Contrary to this intention, a new hierarchical system was developed based on this official rank system. The study of politeness behavior in an official setting offers insight into the interaction between hierarchical structure and social relations in present-day China.

In terms of language use, meetings in an official setting are the best example of a formal and structured interaction. The purpose of a meeting is to carry out activities according to a set agenda. Participants are usually government officials. Though these participants may not know one another well personally, each of them has a clear idea of others' social attributes such as rank, status, and age. In most cases, topics for verbal interaction are pre-determined and known by the participants, and certain rituals have to be followed in the conversation. The discourse features of topic introduction, decision-making, and turn-taking reflect hierarchical behavior based on the power distribution among the participants.

A service encounter represents a different type of speech activity, which is "an instance of face-to-face interaction between a server who is 'officially posted' in some service area and a customer who is present in that service area, that interaction being oriented to the satisfaction of the customer's presumed desire for some service and the server's obligation to provide that service" (Merritt, 1976, p. 321). Interactions in stores, banks, and post offices are typical examples of service encounters. In this type of setting, the institution already sets the topic frame, and the participants have a clear idea of the purpose of their interaction: to carry out the business transaction that the institution is designed to perform. The service person and the customer coordinate in their interaction to reach the shared goal of their encounter.

In China, however, there were two types of service business co-existing in the 1990s: state-run and private businesses. In the early 1950s private businesses were turned into state-run enterprises after the Communist Party took over power in China. As part of the 1979 economic reform, private businesses returned to China's market, and started blooming in the 1990s. These two types of state-run and privately owned businesses are under two different organizational systems. They have a totally different way of doing things and, therefore, produce a great deal of difference in how the service person and the customer deal with each other. The differences will be elaborated in chapters 2 and 3. In short, state-run businesses are a product of the socialist planned economy and are heavily influenced by the Communist ideology. Service people in state-run businesses have appropriated their language style more from the political practice than from the traditional commercial practice, because the traditional way of doing business was abandoned in China after the 1949 Revolution. Service people in the private sector, however, are more business-oriented and motivated to sell. They employ linguistic features that are persuasive and appealing to customers in order to achieve their business goals. Therefore, state-run and private businesses represent two different types of situations. It is important to make this structural distinction because it greatly affects people's politeness behavior, as I will show in chapters 2 and 3.

The family setting is characterized as an informal setting consisting of activities with family members. Conversations in this setting are casual, and topics vary widely. Participants are closely related to one another, but may not be of equal power due to differences in age and status conferred through social practices. This is a situation where intimate relationships are emphasized and talk is mainly for the purpose of maintaining personal relationships or creating solidarity. Family life is often considered to provide the back-stage setting for society, and family is the place where people are most relaxed and casual. While this is certainly true, the traditional hierarchical structure can also be observed in a family setting. The Chinese family represents the oldest state structure in Chinese society as many Chinese scholars point out (for example, Yue, 1989; Zhao & Gao, 1990; Zheng, 1987). When discussing the numerous differences between the Chinese and American family, Hsu (1981) allows that, compared with the four characteristics of discontinuity, exclusiveness, volition, and sexuality of the American family, the Chinese family has the characteristics of continuity (of paternal line), inclusiveness (of many offspring), authority (of the old over the young), and asexuality (little sex between husband and wife, since the primary purpose of their union is to reproduce). Due to these characteristics, hierarchical order, which is often observed in the official setting, is also maintained in the Chinese family. But power may not come from the same source as rank hierarchy in the official setting. Instead, the factors of age and gender carry more weight due to the traditional paternal structure of the family. Participants' linguistic behavior is determined by their roles in this structure.

What I will be emphasizing in the course of the discussion is the link between setting and the use of politeness strategies, explaining how the factors of official rank, age, gender, and knowledge of the addressee's background/social attributes interact and account for linguistic behavior in different settings. According to Goffman (1959), people present themselves relative to the situation they are in. The situation sets up the expectations for people's behavior. My findings support the observation that Chinese tend to employ different politeness strategies depending first on their knowledge of the addressee and then on the situation. For example, due to the asymmetry of power relations in the official setting, the use of politeness strategies is not reciprocal. There are two levels of interpersonal interaction: from the lower to the higher, and from the higher to the lower. Politeness behavior signals these two levels of interaction. Politeness phenomena here reflect the formal end of the politeness continuum suggested by Lakoff (1979). But in a service encounter, when Chinese try to be polite it is the solidarity end of the politeness continuum that is emphasized. So only when we examine politeness behavior in different settings can we have a complete picture of politeness phenomena and the underlying factors for the use of politeness strategies in Chinese culture.

METHODOLOGY AND RESEARCH SITUATION

The research for this study took place over a period of eight years with numerous trips to Mainland China for data collection. Before I personally made my initial research trip to China in early 1991, I asked my friends and family in China to video-tape and audio-tape their verbal interaction in daily life without any specification of situation. I used that material as a pilot study to decide which settings I would like to focus on in my study. I chose service encounters, official meetings, and family gatherings because they represent common situations in daily face-to-face interaction, and a variety of domains from public to private. In early 1991 I spent six weeks doing fieldwork in the cities of Foshan and Guangzhou in the southeastern province of Guangdong.

Foshan is a mid-sized city with a population of about 2,600,000. It was one of the four most famous towns in the Ming (A.D.1368–1644) and Qing (A.D.1616–1911) dynasties, and was known for its porcelain production, handicrafts, silk industry, and agriculture. With China's economic reform in 1979, Foshan's proximity to Hong Kong helped it take the lead in establishing private enterprises and creating business relationships with the outside world, attracting investment and business from Hong Kong, Taiwan and abroad. Since then Foshan's infrastructure, industry, communication, and import and export business have developed rapidly. Foshan is thus considered to be one of the most economically developed and commercially prosperous cities in the country.

Guangzhou is the capital city of Guangdong Province, and one of the biggest cities in China, with a population of about 6,000,000. It is an important political, economic and cultural center for southern China. China's Import and Export Commodities Fair is held in Guangzhou twice a year to promote China's business and trade relationships with the rest of the world. It was also one of the first cities in China to implement the open-door policy in the 1980s and attract foreign investments. Guangzhou's economic development and frequent contacts with the outside world have made it almost a foreign city within China's boundaries. Every year millions of people from inland China rush to Guangzhou to find jobs in a manner reminiscent of the Gold Rush in California in the early 19th century. This migration is referred to as the "Gold Rush to the South" (*nan2 xia4 tao2 jin1*) in China.

The native language of Foshan and Guangzhou is Cantonese, one of eight major dialects in China. Since the government promoted the campaign for a national standardized language in the 1950s, Mandarin has been used in schools and the news media. Frequent business contacts with other parts of China require the natives to deal with people who do not understand Cantonese. Under these circumstances, they have to use Mandarin, the national language. There are also residents who moved to the region from the northern part of China where Mandarin is their native language. So residents of the region, though mainly speakers of Cantonese, can be considered bilingual, especially those of middle-age and younger. For these reasons, my data contain both Mandarin and Cantonese speech. Depending on the speakers and situations, some interactions/conversations are in Mandarin while others are in Cantonese. Sometimes both Mandarin and Cantonese are used in one situation and speakers code-switch between the two dialects. Code-switching refers to the use of more than one language in the course of a single event, or going from one language to the other in mid-speech when both speakers know the language (Saville-Troike, 1989). This is the situation among many Cantonese speakers in Foshan and Guangzhou.

After my initial fieldwork in 1991, I made three subsequent trips to Foshan and Guangzhou from 1992 to 1996 to gather more data and make observations. During my two years of university teaching in Hong Kong from the beginning of 1997 to the end of 1998, I made a number of research trips to these two cities and to other Chinese cities, including Beijing, Nanjing and Kunming. All together this study covers a period of eight years of research and a variety of locations.

My data on service encounters was collected through friends and family networks. One relative of mine introduced me to her colleagues at the bank where she works, which gave me an opportunity to sit at a bank teller's window to observe and audio-tape the interaction between the teller and customers. The clerk in a stamp store was my neighbor many years ago and she allowed me to audio-tape her interaction with customers. I followed my friends and family to shopping malls, wet markets (markets of fresh produce and meats), and street vendors to observe their behavior. The sites for service encounters include banks, post offices, department stores, convenience stores, restaurants, fast food stands, clothing shops, fashion stores, a hospital, and a car dealership. Most interactions were recorded on tapes, some in fieldnotes. All examples used in this book are from transcripts of video- or audio-tapes.

For the official setting, business meetings and job interviews were audio-taped. The business meetings, each lasting from 45 minutes to one hour, included official meetings by different government organizations, bank board meetings, and company business meetings. Because of research restrictions in China, I was not able to be physically present in these meetings. The data was recorded by family and friends, with their permission to use the data for research. I made it clear to them that I was interested in language use, and not the content of the meeting. So they could select a meeting that did not contain sensitive issues. The meetings collected were routine business meetings in the workplace.

Data from family gatherings consists of video-taped and audio-taped family gatherings with two or three generations present. All are middle class urban families with family members working in government organizations or business companies. Occasions for family gatherings include Chinese New Year's Eve dinners, birthday parties, and family reunions.

During my fieldwork, I observed and participated in these activities and asked questions of those who participated in the interaction/conversation to get feedback on the data. I used multiple sources of evidence: first-hand materials, second-hand materials (audio- and video-tapes recorded by other people), direct observation and participant-observation. I also made a special effort to follow the same participants in the different settings of service encounters, the workplace and family interaction to observe situational variation. Quite a few of the participants in my study are present in the data from all three settings. This part of the data will be the main focus for my analysis throughout the book because it provides a base for comparison of politeness behavior across different settings.

ORGANIZATION OF THE BOOK

No matter in which setting an interaction takes place, it is likely that a single factor will be dominant in determining the use of linguistic devices for politeness purposes, though more than one factor may be at work at the same time. My goal is to demonstrate which dimension dominates politeness behavior in various settings within Chinese culture. Chapter 2 and chapter 3 deal with the issue of social distance and how inside and outside relations play a key role in the employment of politeness strategies in Chinese culture. Chapter 2 presents findings from service encounters in state-run stores and shows the interaction patterns distinctive to inside and outside relations. In the public domain of a service encounter, social distance is the main issue in the consideration of politeness strategies. Facework is almost always missing in an outside relationship (for example, when the customer and the salesperson are unacquainted), but often elaborated in an inside relationship (for example, when the customer and the salesperson are acquainted). Facework is performed through discourse elements of opening/closing comments, small talk, and showing involvement. Chapter 3 describes politeness phenomena in a different type of service encounter, that in privately owned stores. In this type of setting, excessive facework is performed by the salesperson to turn the outside relationship into an inside one with the ulterior motive of making a sell. Face strategies used in this setting emphasize the involvement aspect of face want such as building connection, claiming ingroup identity, offering suggestions and engaging in small talk. This confirms the importance of personal relationship in the initial business contact.

Chapter 4 turns our attention to another sociological variable, the power dimension. It examines behavioral patterns in a formal setting, as exemplified by official meetings. I argue that once the type of social relation is settled, the power dimension comes to have a crucial effect. Hierarchical order is defined by the participants' position in the power structure, determined by the power coming from official rank, gender, and age. But not every factor is of equal importance in all situations. These factors override each other in actual face-to-face interaction. The importance of any one social factor is related to the setting in which a speech event takes place. I show that in formal and official settings, official rank dominates linguistic and politeness behavior. The speaker's position in the rank hierarchy determines his/her linguistic choice in politeness behavior. Other factors such as age, gender, and *guanxi* (connection), while important in other domains of Chinese society, are less crucial in the consideration of face strategies in verbal interaction in an official environment.

Chapter 5 focuses on how family members interact with each other and how conversation is organized with regard to the use of politeness strategies. I discuss how the interaction pattern in family gatherings differs from the other two settings in terms of power structure and politeness behavior, using examples from family dinner-table conversations. Among the specific features I examine are topic control, different strategies in responding to men's talk versus women's talk, the ways in which conflict talk is managed, and performance of certain speech acts. I attempt to reveal the interaction of different factors of age seniority, gender, and official rank and answer the questions of which factor contributes most to the power structure that determines the use of face strategies and what are the preferred face strategies in the particular situation of a family gathering.

Based on findings from the analysis of data from each of the three settings, in the concluding chapter (chapter 6) I propose a situation-specific model as an alternative approach to explaining politeness phenomena. The need, as well as the possibility, for an alternative explanation comes from the fact that almost all sociocultural factors such as gender, age, rank, and status are present in all cultures. To understand why people speak the way they do, however, we have to know how much consideration participants give to each factor and where their starting point is. The situation-based approach looks into what social factor weighs most in consideration of the use of politeness strategies in a particular setting in a cultural group and explains cultural differences in terms of relativity and situation variation.

2

"DO I KNOW YOU?" INSIDE AND OUTSIDE RELATIONS IN POLITENESS BEHAVIOR

There is a Chinese story about Zheng Banqiao, a famous Chinese artist and calligrapher of the Qing Dynasty (1616–1911). One day, Zheng dressed like a poor peasant and went to a temple where there were many paintings with Chinese calligraphy. When *Zheng* entered the temple, the monk in charge of greeting guests said "Sit" to him and "Tea" to the temple servant. Then Zheng started looking at the paintings on the wall. When the monk saw that this peasant-like man seemed to be able to understand and enjoy the paintings (a highly respected sign of scholarship), he came up to him and said "Please take a seat," and the order to the servant became "Please serve tea."[1] Only after asking the guest's name did the monk learn that this was the famous Master Zheng who enjoyed high social status because of his highly sought-after painting and calligraphy. Then the monk said to Master *Zheng* with a broad smile, "Please take the honorable seat," and to the servant, "Please serve the best tea." Later the monk asked Zheng to write a couplet to be displayed on the wall to show that the famous Master Zheng had paid a visit to the temple. Zheng thought for a while, and then wrote down, "Sit, please take a

25

seat, please take the honorable seat. Tea, please serve tea, please serve the best tea." Seeing this, the monk felt very embarrassed.

This anecdote criticizes the common practice of judging people based on their clothing. But it also implies a social practice in Chinese culture that ignores the face need of a stranger and applies facework in accordance with the addressee's importance in society. In this story, when the monk first sees Zheng, he takes Zheng for an ordinary person and does not use any face strategies when offering tea. Only when the monk learns the social status of Zheng, does he change his face strategy from a direct blunt command to an elaborate offer filled with polite hedges. So the application of face strategies is the acknowledgment of the addressee's social attributes (for example, age, rank, and status) and the hierarchical difference between the speaker and the addressee (the monk is in a lower social position). If the addressee's social attributes are not revealed, no facework is applied in the interaction.

This raises the question of why the addressee's social attributes are so important in the determination of face strategies. Isn't it true that face strategies are expected to modify a speech act if it is deemed face-threatening? Shouldn't a stranger be treated with some level of politeness? The two encounters cited at the beginning of chapter 1 also indicate the same pattern of behavior: that interaction between total strangers tends to be blunt and abrupt while interaction between acquaintances is filled with extended facework. It is obvious that the social distance between the participants is the first consideration in face-to-face interaction. In this chapter, I shall illustrate the importance of social distance as the first sociological variable in Chinese politeness behavior and show how language use is related to the distinction between inside and outside relations. I shall argue that *guanxi*, the Chinese term for certain kinds of particularistic ties between pairs of people (Tu, 1994), is a dominating factor for politeness behavior in business situations. *Guanxi* results from the emphasis on personal ties and commonality among members of the same group in Chinese culture.

Studies in anthropology, sociology, and history all point out the importance of *guanxi* (personal connection) in Chinese culture. Anthropologist May Mei-hui Yang shows that *guanxi* not only has use-value, but also exchange-value in contemporary China, and that the reliance on established social relationships to get things done has had a long tradition in China. The concept of personal connections is an underlying cultural assumption shared by Chinese everywhere, in Mainland China before and after the Communist Revolution of 1949, in Taiwan, and among overseas Chinese in Southeast Asia, but it has been exalted to everyday practice and a self-conscious discourse with both popular and official forms in the Mainland, especially in the 1980s and the 1990s (Yang, 1994, p. 6). To say that Chinese emphasize *guanxi* does not mean that personal connections are not important in other cultures. It means that *guanxi* in Chinese culture is emphasized to the point that personal connections become a means for meeting the needs and desires of everyday life. The primacy of *guanxi* and binding power of personal relationships are perpetuated in everyday life and consequently in Chinese linguistic politeness as well.

The exploitation of *guanxi* penetrates almost every sphere of social life from getting a house to buying a stamp, from job promotion to school entrance, and from seeing a doctor to getting children admitted to school. It involves families, friends, colleagues, and acquaintances in complex networks of social support in day-to-day life. The art of dealing with and establishing social relationships has become such a large part of the Chinese cultural repertoire and socialization that a person without such a skill would be considered as unfortunate as someone physically handicapped. In his book, Kipnis (1997) describes in detail how the four basic categories of guanxi—family members, relatives, fellow villagers, and friends—are maintained in a rural Chinese village. The exchange of gifts, favors, banquets, and visits embodies the social support and sentimental attachment to *guanxi*.

To understand why personal connection plays such a crucial part in Chinese social relationships, we need to go to the very root of Chinese psychology and mentality. Studies (for example, Bond, 1994; King, 1992) on Asian psychology and social behavior have indicated that Asians make a clear distinction between ingroup and outgroup members, and place great emphasis on group cohesion and interdependence between ingroup members. In traditional China, ingroup members included families, relatives, friends, and fellow villagers. In modern times, fellow schoolmates and fellow colleagues have been added to the ingroup members. Ingroup members form the basic structure for social interaction, and it is within this relationship that elaborate social etiquette is observed and practiced.

As for outgroup members, they are considered temporary contacts not holding any long-term value in the social relationship. Chinese culture is rooted in a kinship-based sedentary agricultural society (Yang, 1994). In traditional rural China, there was little emigration from one place to another. People tended to stay in one location all their lives and thus formed strong ties with family members and fellow villagers. Newcomers to the village were taken as a threat to group cohesion and often cast out by the locals. It took a long time for newcomers to overcome the boundary of inside and outside relations and establish social relationships in the new place. If there was some personal connection to introduce the outsider to the locals, such as that he/she was someone's cousin's cousin, it was easier for him/her to be accepted.

Because of this social practice of making a strict distinction between inside and outside relations, personal connections have become an important medium in all sorts of social interactions, ranging from official to business and personal activities. Personal connection can be seen as breaking the ice between the inside and outside, but it is used to such an extent that it has the power to gain special privileges, and has use-value and exchange value. The value of *guanxi* really comes from the social practice of *nei wai you bie* (distinguishing between the inside and the outside).

When it comes to language use, something as simple as topic introduction is determined by the type of relationship between the participants. Scollon and Scollon (1991) found that in face-to-face interaction, topic initiation is based on the task in an outside relation, while in an inside relation the topic is introduced by the person who is in a higher position in the hierarchical structure. For example, in shops it is a temporary task-oriented relationship. Usually customers initiate the encounter and often begin directly with the topic: "Firepot for four," or "Three air-mail stamps," and the server often takes care of several customers at once. On a school campus, on the other hand, the student will wait for the professor to introduce the conversation topic. This indicates that the distinction between inside and outside relations has permeated and is perpetuated in the cultural tools of language.

Linguistic politeness is part of language use and social practice. It no doubt encodes the inside and outside distinction in Chinese culture. In other words, the sociological variable of social distance has an essential role in the consideration of face strategies. The first step in face-to-face interaction is to measure the social distance between the two participants: whether they are acquainted, how long they have been acquainted, how well they know each other, and how close they are. If they are perceived as in an outside relationship, they are not considered to be in the system for face concern. When they are in an inside relation, efforts are made to build and cultivate personal connections.

In this chapter we will see how this works. I will show in detail interactions that have taken place in service encounters. A service encounter is perceived as an outside relation in Chinese culture, because the server and the customer come into contact for just a short time, and the relationship is temporary and task-oriented. Language use is limited and functions to facilitate the business transaction. Coupled with the concept of outside relation in service encounters is the socialist practice in Mainland China under the Communist rule. The development of China's service industry has been greatly affected by the political situation under the Communist rule. Shortly after the Communist Party of China took power in 1949, drastic and large-scale social reform was launched in every sphere of society, including the service industry. The state-run business was the result of China's socialist reform campaign (1955–1958) to transform private into state-run business under the socialist planned economy system (cf. Yu, 1989). During this campaign, Chinese government bought out or closed down most of privately owned stores and turned them into state-run stores or cooperatives. Private stores very soon disappeared from the society. For the next 30 years, all service businesses were run by the state with a socialist ideology of self-service and equality between the server and the customer. Salespersons were employed by the state and received a monthly salary regardless of the sales volume they made. Due to the scarcity of almost any kind of consumer goods in those days and the lack of motivation on the part of the service people to serve, customers had to fight for attention and service from salespersons, who on the whole were quite reluctant to help customers in any situation. The practice of self-service in service industries was also emphasized as an indoctrination of socialist ideology during that time. The shortage of any kind of merchandise also caused a high demand for service in stores as customers crowded around the counter shouting for the salesperson's attention. As a result, service encounters were often considered cold business interactions.

In the following sections I shall focus on one state-run store to give a detailed analysis of the interaction pattern between the clerk and customers and face strategies applied in these interactions. This stamp store is a sub-branch of the postal service operated by the state, specializing in selling commemorative stamps. The clerks working there are government employees, receiving a fixed monthly salary. At the time I recorded interactions in the store, there was one female clerk in her 30s sitting behind the counter inside which stamps were displayed. There was a partition separating the clerk from the customers. When customers came in to look at or buy stamps, they had to ask the clerk to take the stamps out from under the counter. All together 24 customers (including two couples) visited the store. Among them two were acquainted with the clerk. One was her former neighbor, and the other was one of her supervisors. All the interactions were in Cantonese, except one in which the clerk spoke to her former neighbor in Mandarin, a language they have shared since childhood.

TASK-ORIENTED INTERACTION
IN AN OUTSIDE RELATION

A distinction can be made between acquainted customers and unacquainted customers, because there are noticeable differences in the ways a server interacts with an acquainted and an unacquainted customer. With an unacquainted customer, the interaction focuses on the task and can be characterized as terse, brief, and abrupt, with minimum politeness strategies to mitigate FTAs or to enhance the face of the other. The interaction consists of a sequence of opening, request for service, transaction, and closing. At each stage, we can observe how much facework is applied in interaction in an outside relationship by looking at linguistic features used by the participants.

Opening of the Interaction

It is a common practice in a Western service encounter that the opening of the interaction is initiated by the server who usually signals his/her availability either by verbal expression: "May I help you?" or by looking up in expectation (cf. Merritt, 1976). But in this Chinese stamp store, it was a common scene for a customer to walk into the store and come up to the counter to look for stamps. The clerk in the stamp store was reading a book and sometimes talking to me (I was sitting behind

TABLE 2.1.   Number and Syntactic Structures of the
First Utterance in Service Encounters in the Stamp Store ($N = 22$)

Syntax	First utterance by customers	First utterance by the clerk
Question	27%	9%
Question with PM*	23%	
You-imperative		4.5%
Basic imperative	32%	
Statement		4.5%
Total	82%	18%

Note: *PM = politeness markers, including such words or phrases as formulaic polite expressions, politeness hedges, and address forms.

the counter, next to her) between serving customers. The clerk rarely acknowledged the arriving customers. So customers had to get her attention and make the first move to get service. Interactions in this stamp store are mostly initiated by customers. The first utterance made by customers was, in most cases, a direct request for service or a question asking for information or service. Table 2.1 shows the number and syntactic structures of the first utterance by the server and customers.

As Table 2.1 shows, most of the first moves are made by customers. Of the 22 interactions, 18 (82 percent) are initiated by customers, while only four (18 percent) are initiated by the clerk. Of the four instances in which the clerk makes the first move, two are interactions with acquaintances. The other two cases are when the customer has been inside the store for some time without making the initial move. Then the clerk asks what the customer wants in a very blunt way (for example, "What do you want? Speak up"). Usually, the lack of initial acknowledgment from the server forces the customer to make the first move. The customer's request, however, is as blunt as the clerk's question.

> ***Example 2.1.***   Customer #13—male, 20s
> (The man approaches the counter)
>
> 1. C#13:   *Bei2 loeng5 zong1 go2 di1 ming4 seon3 pin3.*
>   give two MW^2 those postcards
>
>   Give me two of those postcards.
>
> 2. Clerk: *Jat1 tou3 deng6 hai6 loeng5 zoeng1?*
>   one set or two MW
>
>   One set or two?
>
> 3. C#13:   *Jat1 tou3.*
>   one set

One set.

4. Clerk: *Jat1 tou3 saam1 hou4.*
one set three dime

Thirty cents for one set.

5. C#13:   *Saam1 hou4.*
three dime

Thirty cents.

(C#13 pays the money, and the clerk gives him the postcards)

In this interaction, the customer makes the first move by making a request (line 1, "Give me two of those postcards"). The request is in the form of an imperative and is not hedged with any face redressive devices. This kind of direct request is frequently used in the first utterance by a customer to ask for service. It seems to be the norm that customers are expected to give information as to what they want from the clerk. If this norm is violated, that is, when customers do not make the first move for some time, then the clerk makes the first move, also without any facework. There are two instances in which the clerk makes the first move. Example 2.2 is an interaction between the clerk and a male customer.

Example 2.2.   C#20—male, 30s, approaches the counter while the clerk is talking to the researcher. He hesitates a little.

1. Clerk: *Jiu1 mat1 je5, nei5 gong2 laa1.*
want what you speak TW[3]

What do you want? Speak up.

2. C#20:   … (inaudible)

3. Clerk: *Baat3 baat3 nin4 go3 bou6 aa1?*
eighty year MW album QW[4]

Stamp album for '88?

4. C#20:   *Aa1.*
TW

Yeah.

(The clerk goes to look for the stamp album)

The customer did not make the first move when he came in, probably because he saw the clerk was talking to someone. After some time, the clerk signaled her availability by asking the customer to tell her what he wanted (line 1, "What do you want? Speak up"). It is interesting to observe that instead of offering help by saying something like "Can I help you?" which is usually found to be the first utterance in an American service encounter, the clerk used a directive requesting the customer to provide information.

The opening of an interaction is quite important in politeness phenomena because it sets the tone of the whole interaction. The first utterance we encounter affects the way we proceed in the situation, for we are likely to form our expectation of what sort of encounter it will be based on the first utterance. The use of politeness strategies is, in most situations, reciprocal in nature. If the encounter has a friendly opening, we tend to continue the friendly atmosphere by employing face strategies that mitigate the imposition of face-threatening acts. If it is a cold and task-oriented encounter, we then adjust our expectations and use linguistic strategies that correspond to it.

Closing of the Encounter

As shown above, the opening of the encounter in an outside relationship is normally initiated by the customer in a direct and terse way. At the end of the encounter, it is as abrupt as the opening and lacks any ritual linguistic expression for the closing of interaction. The last utterance is made by the clerk to tell customers how much they have to pay, and there is no verbal exchange of formal ending to a service encounter. In contrast to American culture where both the server and the customer are expected to say "Thank you" and maybe "Goodbye" or "Have a nice day" to close the encounter, in a Chinese service encounter, the closing is completed (via server) when the action (without words) of the encounter is finished. The clerk gives the customer the requested item and the customer pays the money. The interaction is thus completed without exchange of ritual facework from either the server or the customer.

Consider the following example in which the customer (a teenage male) is buying new commemorative stamps. The last utterance in the interaction is a request from the clerk.

Example 2.3.   Customer #8—male, teenager

    1. C#8:   *Nei1 go3 gei2 zin2?*
        this MW how-much money

        How much is this?

    2. Clerk: *Nei1 di1? Saam1 hou4.*
        these three dime

        These? Thirty cents.

    3.   *Hoi1 zo2 san1 kaat1 mei6 nei5?*
        open GW[5] new card not you

Have you opened up a new card?[6]

4. C#8:   *Mou4.*
no

No.

5. Clerk: *Hoi1 m4 hoi1?*
open not open

Do you want one?

6. C#8:   *Hoi1.*
open

Yes.

7. Clerk: *Gau3 m4 gau3 zin2? Ng5 man1 bun3 jat1 go3.*
enough not enough money five dollars half one MW

Do you have enough money? Five and a half yuan each.

8. C#8:   *Gau3 ge2.*
enough GW

Yes, I have enough.

9. Clerk: *Luk2 man1 cat1 hou4 jat1.*
six dollar seven dime one

Six yuan and seventy-one cents.

10. C#8:   *Nei1 di1 ne1?*
these QW

How about these?

11. Clerk: *Gau3 laa1. Jat1 fan1 jau5 mou4?*
enough GW one cent have not

That's enough. Do you have one cent?

12. C#8:   *Mou4.*
no

No.

13. Clerk: *Bei2 jat1 fan1 ngo5.*
give one cent me

(Obviously didn't hear C#8)
Give me one cent.

> (C#8 doesn't have one cent requested by the clerk. So he just shakes
> his head. The clerk then gives the card and stamps to C#8, who pays
> the money. The clerk gives him the change. The encounter ends.)

The last utterance in the exchange is a request from the clerk, which is also the last utterance in the encounter. Then there is some exchange of body language (the customer shakes his head) and the action of handing the stamps and the money. The interaction thus ends without any expression of politeness rituals, such as "thank you" or "good-bye." The verbal interaction does not even extend to the end of the action being performed.

Of the 22 verbal interactions between the clerk and customers, nine (41 percent) end with the clerk telling customers how much they have to pay; five (23 percent) end with the clerk answering a question from a customer; three (13.5 percent) are requests made by the clerk to ask customers to give her small change; another three (13.5 percent) end with customers' repetition of what the clerk has told them (either of the price or of the availability of goods); and two (9 percent) interactions are interrupted by another customer.[7] The verbal interaction in service encounters is only part of an action structure (Schiffrin's term, 1987). Handing the money to the clerk and handing the stamps to customers is the two-part end of the encounter. Since the main task of the encounter is to get things done, language is used to assist the process of the transaction rather than to exchange information or to create social relationships. Once the goal of their encounter is made clear to both parties, they do not have to use any politeness strategies to accomplish that goal. Thus, at the closing of the encounter, no politeness ritual is observed.

Request and Compliance

A service encounter generally consists of an opening of the encounter, request for service, compliance with the request, transaction, and closing. In discussing the generic structure potential of service encounters, Ventola (1987) believes that sale request, sale compliance, sale, purchase, and purchase closure are the obligatory elements of service encounters. Here, request and compliance makes up the essential part of a service encounter. The purpose of a request, as a speech act, is to get the addressee to perform a future act to the benefit of the speaker (Searle, 1976). Requests thus place an imposition on the addressee. If the speaker does not want to sound pushy, he/she can redress the imposition of an FTA by applying face strategies such as indirectness or politeness hedges. For instance a pre-request (Heringer's term, 1977) preceding a request to check the willingness and availability of the addressee reduces the harshness of a request. Also a request phrased in the form of a question is less imposing than a request in the form of an imperative. Merritt (1976, 1984) found that in American service encounters, customers' requests are often phrased in the form of a question, and servers comply by giving a verbal acknowledgment of the request and then performing the act.

In Chinese service encounters, however, requests are often performed in the form of a basic imperative (verb and object), such as "Give me one stamp," or "Show me that sweater." Requests made by both the server and the customer lack politeness hedges. In the following sequence of interaction, both the customer and clerk make requests, and there is similarity in structure between the requests.

Example 2.4.   Customer #7—female, teenager

   1. C#7:   *Bei2 jat1 zung2, bei2 loeng5 zung2 siu2 jan4*
            give one MW give two MW little people

   2.   *gwok3, jat1 joeng5 jat1 zung2*
            kingdom one kind one MW

            Give me one, give me two of the Little Kingdom, one of each kind.

   3. Clerk: *Loeng5 zung2 aa1?*
            two MW QW

            Two?

   4. C#7:   *Hai6.*
            yes

            Yes.

   5. Clerk: *Jat1 joeng6 loeng5 zung2?*
            one kind two MW

            Two of each kind?

   6. C#7:   *Jat1 joeng6 jat1 zung2*
            one kind one MW

            One of each kind.

   7. Clerk: *Jat1 joeng6 jat1 zung2*
            one kind one MW

            One of each kind.

   8. C#7:   *Gaa3 muk6 biu2 jik6 bei2 aa1.*
            Price list also give GW

            Give me the price list, too.

   9. Clerk: *Bei2 zoeng1 gaa3 muk6 biu2. Jat1 man1 jat1 hou4 Jat1*
            give GW price list. one dollar one dime one.

  10.   *Saam1 hou4, gau2 hou4, loeng5 man1 sei3 hou4 jat1.*
            three dime nine dime two dollar four dime one.

  11.   *Bei2 jat1 fan1 ngo5*
            give one cent me

TABLE 2.2. Percentage of Requests in Different
Syntactic Forms in the State-Run Stamp Store

Syntactic form	Number	Percentage
Statement	1	4.2%
Basic imperative	18	75%
Imperative + PM[*]	2	8.3%
Question	3	12.5%
Total	24	100%

Note: [*]PM = politeness markers

> You want the price list. One yuan and twenty-one cents, thirty
> cents, ninety cents, two yuan and forty-one cents. *Give me one
> cent.*

12. C#7:   *Hou2*
            okay

            Okay.

            (The customer takes out one cent)

13. Clerk: *Jat1 man1 loeng5 hou4 jat1.*
              one dollar two dime one

              One yuan and twenty-one cents.

There are three requests in this interaction: two made by the customer (lines
1–2, and line 8), and one by the clerk (line 11). Interestingly, they all share identical features: the same syntactic structure—verb & object imperative form; the
same verb "give"; no politeness marker used with the requests. But the interaction proceeds smoothly. Both interlocutors comply with what is being requested;
in line 3 the clerk asks a question to clarify the customer's needs and then
repeats the customer's request in line 7 just to make sure. When the clerk
requests the customer to give her one cent (line 11) the customer complies with
a verbal acknowledgment ("OK") as well as the action (gives her one cent).

This type of request in the form of a direct imperative is very common in service
encounters in state-run stores. Table 2.2 is a summary of the percentage of
requests made in the exchanges between the stamp store clerk and her customers.

The most prevalent form for requests is the basic imperative, while politeness
markers are used in only two (8.3 percent) instances (by women customers). Questions, usually softening the imposition of a request, are not used very often either
(only 12.5 percent). This indicates that in an outside relation situation like a service encounter, face concern is not a major issue. Neither the server nor the cus-

tomer attends to the face of the other person. The participants in an outside relationship do not acknowledge a need to reduce the imposition of a request. Because face is considered an interrelational concern in Chinese culture (Chang & Holt, 1994), when no interrelation is established between the two participants in a situation, face concern is reduced to the minimum. This is exactly the case in a service encounter. The expected norm of behavior for both the clerk and customers is to follow Gricean maxims in conversation (Grice, 1975), in other words, to focus on the efficiency of the interaction. The main strategy is bald on-record (Brown and Levinson's term, 1987). I call this type of interaction a task-oriented interaction. That is, the interpersonal relationship is not the focus here. The interlocutors come into contact because of the task that they have to fulfill. There is only minimal use of verbal as well as politeness expressions.

Another phenomenon worth discussing is that when the act being requested is completed, the requester does not give any verbal expression of appreciation or gratitude. This seems to be the norm in all cases when requests are made. Let's look at the following segment of an interaction:

Example 2.5.   Customer #26—female, 30s

1. C#26:   *Bei2 di1 jan4 man4 bai6 jau4 piu3.*
give some people money stamp

Give me some Chinese money stamps.

2. Clerk: *Jat1 man1 ji6 hou4 jat1.*
one dollar two dime one

One yuan and twenty-one cents.

(The clerk starts talking to someone else, then comes back to talk to C#26, who gives the clerk a one-yuan note and a fifty-cent note)

3. Clerk: *Jau5 mou4 jat1 fan1*
have not one cent

Do you have one cent?

4. C#26:   *Naa4*
there

Here.

5. Clerk: *Bei2 faan1 saam1 hou4*
give back three dime

Here is your change of thirty cents.

(End of the encounter)

Two actions are being requested and then completed in this exchange. First, the customer makes a request for a special stamp (line 1) and the clerk sells her the stamps (line 5). The clerk makes the second request asking the customer for small change (one cent, line 3) to save herself the trouble of looking for one cent, and the customer complies. But in neither case is appreciation for the co-operation shown verbally. Both interlocutors are concentrating on the task of their encounter rather than showing concern for face.

Although the merchandise sold in this state-run store (commemorative stamps and stamps album) is highly impersonal and may not lead to conversation that involves more personal interest (such as color, style and size of a dress), examples from other state-run stores selling personal items yield a pattern similar to the one in the stamp store described in this section. For instance, one woman customer went to a women's clothing section in a state-run department store to buy sweaters (the same merchandise sold in a private store, as I am going to discuss in the following chapter). The server there showed an identical pattern of behavior.

> ***Example 2.6.***   Customer is in the women's clothing section, looking at sweaters. The shop clerk (30s) is standing behind the counter, chatting with her co-worker. The interaction is in Cantonese.

> 1. Customer: (pointing at the sweaters on display)

>   *Bei2 ngo5 go1 gin6 laang5 saam1 tai2 haa5*
>   give me that MW sweater look once

>   Give me that sweater to look at.

>   (The clerk takes down the sweater. Customer looks at it)

> 2. Customer: *Jau5 mou4 daai6 di1 gaa3?*
>   have not larger GW

>   Do you have a larger size?

>   (The clerk shakes her head.)

> 3. Customer: (pointing at another sweater on display)

>   *Go2 gin6 ne1?*
>   that one QW

>   How about that one?

> 4. Clerk: *Go2 gin6 zung6 sai3 aa1.*
>   that one even small TW

>   That one is even smaller!

5. Customer: *Nei1 gin6 gei2 zin2?*
            this one how-much money

            How much is this one?

6. Clerk: *Gau2 sap6 baat3 man1.*
            ninety eight dollar

            Ninety-eight dollars.

            (Customer gives the clerk one hundred dollars. The clerk gives the customer the sweater and the change. End of encounter)

This encounter follows a pattern very similar to that in the encounters between the stamp store clerk and the customers with whom she is unacquainted. The customer makes the first move by asking the clerk to show her the sweater (line 1). The clerk does not say anything, but just takes out the sweater for the customer to see. When the customer asks if there is a larger size, the clerk simply shakes her head. Only when the customer points at another sweater and challenges the validity of the clerk's reply (line 3) does the clerk make her first utterance in the encounter, after the customer has already taken up three turns. The closing is similar to that in the stamp store, too—only the action is performed and no verbal exchange is made between the clerk and the customer. In short, it is not the type of merchandise sold in the store that limits the verbal interaction. What counts most are the setting and interpersonal relationships between interlocutors. If we look at the interaction between the clerk in the stamp store and her acquainted customers, we will see a difference in politeness behavior.

Use of Politeness Markers

Politeness markers are formulaic expressions in a language that hedge an utterance to reduce its imposition. There are elaborate formulaic expressions in the Chinese language to address a variety of situations and addressees, such as other-elevating and self-degrading strategies like *gui xing* (your honorable family name) versus *xiao xing* (my small family name), *fu shang* (your honorable residence) versus *han she* (my humble residence) to show respect and deference to the addressee. These formulaic expressions encode a cultural value that emphasizes the hierarchical order between the participants in that the other is placed in a higher position and the self is put in a lower one. The use of politeness markers reflects an unequal status between the participants. In a situation in which the hierarchical order is not clearly defined such as a service encounter, when to apply politeness markers to an utterance becomes questionable. In my data collected in state-run service businesses, formulaic politeness expressions were rarely used. For example, of the 22 interactions in the stamp store, there were only two interactions in which the customer used formulaic politeness expressions, and in both cases, the customers were women. One woman customer used the phrase *cing2man6* (may I ask …) as in the following example:

Example 2.7.   Customer #21—female 20s

1. C#21:   *Cing2 man6, jau5 mou4 jau4 piu3 kaat1 maai6?*
please ask have not stamp card sell

May I ask, do you sell stamp cards?

2. Clerk: *Jau5 gau6 kaat1 zau6 jau5, mou4 gau6 kaat1 zau6 mou4.*
have old card then have, no old card then not

If you have the old card, (you) can get the new one, if not, you can't have it.

(The customer walks away.)

In the second encounter, another woman used a kinship term of address (Auntie) and the formulaic phrase *mgoi* (sorry to bother you) to make her request:

Example 2.8.   C#20—female, 20s

1. C#20:   *Aa3 ji4, m4 goi1 zoi3 bei2 jat1 bun3 go1 go3.*
auntie sorry-to-bother-you again give one MW that MW

Auntie, *sorry to bother you.* Give me one of those.

2. Clerk: *Jau4 piu3 gaa3 muk6 biu2?*
stamp price list

The stamp price list?

3. C#20:   *M4*
TW

Yeah.

(The clerk shows the customer the stamp price list)

In the above two cases, the female customer phrases her request by a formulaic polite expression ("May I ask," or "Sorry to bother you"), which is not found in most customers' requests, particularly male customers' requests. Another politeness marker is the kinship address term "auntie" used by customers to address the clerk. The extended use of kinship terms in Chinese to address nonkinship interactants is a way of showing respect if the addressee is older, or showing friendliness and closeness if the addressee is of the same age or younger (Chao, 1976; Zhao & Gao, 1990). Therefore the use of kinship terms with nonkin operates as a politeness strategy. However, of the 22 unacquainted customers in the stamp store, only 5 (22 percent) of them, teenagers or female customers, use the address form *aa ji* (auntie). In short, formulaic politeness expressions are not a common feature of interactions in this type of service encounter. As for the clerk, she doesn't use any politeness markers at all in any her speech. The limited usage of politeness markers in this kind of service encounter indicates the participants' perception of the nature of the interaction and the type of social relationship.

The use of politeness markers corresponds to the power relation; if the speaker is in a lower power position than the addressee, he/she tends to be deferential to the addressee by using politeness markers. In this situation, the addressee is the clerk, who possesses institutionalized power, and the customer has to request a favor from her in rendering the service. In socialist state-run businesses, there is a reversed power relation between the server and the customer. The lack of competition and scarcity of commodities give the salesperson a special privilege to control certain types of goods. A salesperson can use this privilege to cultivate his/her personal connections and sell certain things to his/her acquaintances in exchange for other kinds of personal favors. With the unacquainted customer, however, there is no exchange value in the temporary contact, so the salesperson is not motivated to serve. The customer, then, is in a less privileged position. That is why not much effort is made by the salesperson to ensure a smooth interaction through the use of politeness markers.

RELATIONSHIP-BASED INTERACTION IN AN INSIDE RELATION

In Chinese culture inside relations refer to family, relatives, friends, and fellows from the same town, same school, and same workplace. This relation extends to include the social network of acquaintances through which one obtains material and political gains in socialist China. Yang (1994) shows that personal connections *(guanxi)* in China have use-value as well as exchange-value developed through China's contemporary history of political upheaval (for example, the Cultural Revolution of 1966–1976) and economic changes (for example, economic reform started in 1979). During the Cultural Revolution, when everything in the society was under rigid control, people relied on *guanxi* to get entrance to some job positions or for political gain. Since the economic reforms launched in 1978 at the Third Plenary of the Eleventh Party Congress, the Chinese economy has turned away from a state-planned economy toward a more free market economy. The use of *guanxi* has also turned from the political exchange of opportunities to a materialist exchange of usable goods, and entered the market forces (Yang, 1994, p. 159).

During the time when I was recording interactions in the stamp store, two of the clerk's acquaintances arrived. One was her former neighbor, and the other was the chairman of the labor union of her company. These two encounters reveal obvious differences from the interactions with customers with whom she was unacquainted. With customers she knew, the clerk offered to help, and was inclined to give detailed explanations and suggestions. Special attention was paid to face concern and maintaining the personal connections. Linguistic strategies employed showed effort on the part of both parties to be involved in the relationship and give face to each other. Consider the following segment of the interaction between the clerk and her former neighbor:

Example 2.9.   C#5—female, 30s, former neighbor of the clerk. C#5 brings her 10-year-old daughter to the store. The interaction is in Mandarin.

1. C#5:   *Chunzhi.*
Chunzhi

Chunzhi.

2. Clerk: *Ei4, ni3 lai2 le.*
hey you come GW

Oh, hey, you've come.

3. Daughter:(to Mother) *Wo3 xi3 huan1 nei4 ge4 ming2 xing4 pian4.*
I like that MW post-card

I like those postcards.

(The daughter points at two postcards on display)

4. Clerk: *Na2 liang3 ge4?*
which two MW

Which two?

5. C#5:   *Na4 liang3 ge4.*
that two MW

Those two.

(exchanges between C#5 and her daughter)

6. Clerk: *Liang3 kuai4 wu3, you3 mei2 you3?*
two dollar fifth have not have

Do you have two dollars and fifty cents?

7. C#5:   *You3 wa.*
have tw

Yes, I do.

8. Clerk: *Gei3 liang3 kuai4 wu3 wo3.*
give two dollar fifty me

Give me two dollars and fifty cents.

9. C#5:   *Hai2 yao4 liang3 ge4 xiao3 yang2 ming2 xing4 bian4.*
also want two MW little goat postcard

I'd also like to have two of the postcards with little goats.

10. Clerk: *Xiao3 yang2, deng3 yi1 xia4 la. Na4 ge4 san1 mao2.*
little goat wait a-while TW that one three dime

The one with little goats… Just a minute. That one is thirty cents.

11. C#5:   *Hao3.*
Okay

Okay.

12. Clerk: *Ni3 gei3 liang3 kuai4 wu3 wo3. Ni3 hai2 shi4 …*
you give two dollar fifty me. you still be …

Give me two dollars and fifty cents. You also … (inaudible)

13. C#5:   *Na4 ge4 shi4 san1, san1 kuai4 qian2.*
that MW be three three dollar money

That's three, three dollars.

14. Clerk: *Xing2. Liang3 kuai4 wu3.*
OK two dollar fifty

15.   *Wo3 zhao3 ni3 er4 shi2 wu3 ah. En, gao3 zhei4 me san3.*
I give you twenty-five TW TW do such change

16.   *Zhei4 ge4 you2 pao4 jiu4 shi4 er4 shi2 kuai4 wu3.*
this MW stamp just be twenty dollar fifty

17.   *Ni3 jiu4 gei2 le wo3 liang3 kuai4 wu3.*
you just give GW me two dollar fifty

18.   *Jiu4 shou1 ni3 shi2 kuai4 qian2 jiu4 xing2 le.*
only accept you ten dollar money just OK GW

19.   *Jiu4 shuo1 zhei4 liang3 ka3 jiu4 shou1 hui2 ta1.*
just say this two card just take-back it

20.   *Sheng4 le san1 ge4 ka3,*
leave GW three MW card

21.   *hai2 you3 san1 ge4 ka3.*
still have three MW card

22.   *Yi1 ge4 ka3 jiu4 wu3 kuai4, hai2 you3 shi2 wu3 kuai4.*
        one MW card just five dollar still have ten five dollar

        Yes. Two dollars and fifty cents.
        I'll give you twenty-five dollars change. Eh, that's a lot of change.
        These stamps are twenty dollars and fifty cents.
        You gave me two dollars and fifty cents.
        I'll just take ten dollars from you.
        That's to say, I'll get back these two cards.
        There are still three cards left.
        There are still three cards.
        Each is worth five dollars. So there are still fifteen dollars.

The clerk and C#5 were former neighbors and playmates in their childhood. Mandarin is the language they have shared since they were children. To show the inside relationship between them, the clerk switched to Mandarin when C#5 addressed her by her given name, *Chunzhi,* in Mandarin. C#5 is fluent in Cantonese, too, but she uses the language that they shared since childhood to show camaraderie. Then the clerk cuts in (line 4) when C#5 and her daughter are talking to each other. This is a friendly gesture to offer help and show attention to the customer. When C#5 makes a request for postcards (line 9), the clerk repeats C#5's request and asks her to wait while she is busy counting the money. Line 14 to 22 is her monologue containing a detailed explanation of how much the customer has to pay, how she came up with the figure, and how much is left in C#5's account. All these linguistic features—choosing the language that expresses the length of their acquaintance, offering help, repeating what the other says and giving details—are ways of showing involvement and creating rapport between the interlocutors (Tannen, 1989).

Another noticeable feature in the encounter with acquainted customers is that the interaction is longer, with small talk before and after the transaction itself. Small talk, as Brown and Levinson put it, is "where the subject of talk is not as important as the fact of carrying on a conversation" (1987, p. 109). It is a way to claim common ground between the speaker and the hearer—common concerns and common attitudes toward interesting events. Coupland, Robinson, and Coupland notice that some forms of "small talk" are designed phatically, and that there are "two essential functional characteristics for phatically designed talk: the relative foregrounding of socio-relational goals over informational and task goals, and a relative lowering of commitment to openness, factuality and the ideational significance of utterances" (1994, p. 92). Along this line, phatic talk is a kind of face-work in interpersonal interaction used by the clerk and customers with whom she is acquainted to consolidate the existing social relationship between them. The following sequence is part of the interaction between the clerk and the chairman of her labor union. It starts with a certain amount of phatic talk before they finally get to the main topic:

Example 2.10.   Customer #24—male, 50s, chairman of the labor union of the stamp company

1. Clerk:
Wai3, nei5 go3 zai2 faan1 lai4 naa4?
hi your son return TW

Hi, is your son back?

2. C#24:
Faan1 laa1.
back TW

Yes.

3. Clerk:
Haa2?
ah

What?

4. C#24:
Faan1 laa1.
back TW

Yes, he's back.

5. Clerk:
Haa2? Fuk6 jyun4 la?
ah retire (from army) TW

Oh, retired from the army?

6. C#24:
Faan1 lai4.
return

He's back.

7. Clerk:
Hai6 m4 hai6 fuk6 jyun4 laa1?
be not be retire (from army) TW

Is he retired from the army?

8. C#24:
Hai6 aa1. Aa3 ng5 gam1 jat6 mou4 faan1?
yes TW Ah Ng today not back

Yes. Is Ah Ng back today?

9. Clerk:
Aa3 ng5 gam1 jat6 san4 zou2 gin3 dou1 keoi5.
Ah Ng today morning see him

Yes, I saw him this morning.

(There are eight more exchanges of the small talk about Ah Ng and somebody else)

10. C#24:
Sou2 jat6 fung1 dou3 zo2 mei6?
first - day-of-issue arrive GW not

Have you got the first-day-of-issue (stamps)?

The relationship between C#24 and the clerk is perceived as an inside one with a superior-subordinate hierarchy. Thus the clerk, as the one in the lower position, makes the first move by asking about the Chairman's son (line 1). And the chairman asks about another person (Ah Ng) whom they both know. This small talk goes on for a few seconds before the chairman makes his request to buy stamps (line 10). Even though both the clerk and the customer know quite well the expected goal of their encounter—to sell/buy stamps—they engage in small talk before the customer brings up the topic of wanting to see some first-day-of-issue stamps. Scollon and Scollon (1995) describe this pattern of topic introduction as the inductive pattern following a "call-answer-facework-topic" sequence in contrast to the deductive pattern of introducing the topic initially. In the inductive pattern of topic introduction, the social relationship is taken into consideration and participants wait for the right moment to bring up the topic by engaging in a period of facework.

Since *guanxi* is such an important aspect of Chinese social interaction, emphasis on relatedness and closeness becomes part of facework in service encounters. The following excerpt is the continuation of their interaction in which the chairman asks for more stamps and the clerk emphasizes the inside relationship between them.

Example 2.11.   C#24—male, 50s, chairman of the labor union of the stamp company

1. C#24:   *Bei2 do1 tiu4 ngo5.*
give more roll me

Give me one more roll (of stamps)

2. Clerk: *Jau6 jiu1 bei2 do1 tiu4 nei5. Waang4 kaat1 mou4 dak1 lo2.*
again need give more roll you horizontal card not can get

3.   *Gwaan1 zyu3 nei5 aa1. Dim2 aa1?*
care-about you TW why TW

4.   *Zung6 soeng2 dim2 joeng6.*
still want how

Give you another roll.
There's no horizontal card.
I'm doing you a favor.
What? What else do you want?

5. C#24:   *Dim2 aa1? Waang4 kaat1 mou4 dak1 lo2.*
why TW horizontal card not can get

Why? There's no horizontal card?

6. Clerk: *Hai6, dou1 zo saam1 fan6 zi1 jat1 piu3.*
yes come GW three share GW one stamp

7.	*Zung6 jau5 gei2 do1 wa.*
	still have how-many TW

	Eh, only one-third of the stamps arrived.
	How many do you think are left?

8. C#24:	*Dou1 zo2 saam1 fan6 zi1 jat1 piu3.*
	come GW three share GW one stamp

	One-third of the stamps arrived.

→9. Clerk:	*Jau5 ge3, ci5 nei5 gam2 joeng6 zau2 hau6 mun4 ge3 sin1 jau5.*
	have GW like you such go back door GW then have

	Yes, only people like you who come through the "backdoor"
	can have (stamps).

10. C#24:	*Hai6 m4 hai6 gaa3?*
	be not be TW

	Is that so?

→11. Clerk:	*Ou3, dong1 jin4 laa1.*
	oh certainly GW

12.	*Nei5 tai2 tung1 zi1 ji5ging1 ceot1 lai4 laa1.*
	you look announcement already out come GW

13.	*Lau4 faan1 jat1 di1. M4 hou2 jat1 tou3 dou1 mou 4.*
	save some no good one set all have-not

14.	*Lau4 faan1 bei2 guk6 zoeng2 maa3, hai6 m4 hai6?*
	save for bureau - head TW be not be

	Oh, of course.
	Look, the announcement is already up there.
	I have to save some. I can't sell all of them.
	Have to save some for the Bureau Head, right?

15. C#24:	*Gei2 do1 zin2?*
	how-much money

	How much (do I owe you)?

16. Clerk:	*Sap6 man1, sap6 ng5. Nei1 dou6 loeng5 man1 bad1,*
	ten dollar fifteen here two dollar eight

17.	*sap6 cat1 man1 baat3. Gai3 jat1 haa5 hai6 m4 hai6.*
	seventeen dollar eight calculate once be not be

> Ten yuan, fifteen yuan, this one, two yuan and eighty cents,
> seventeen yuan and eighty cents. Add it up yourself and see if
> it is right.

18. C#24:   *Nei1 go3 loeng5 man1 baat3.*
this one two dollar eight

This one's two yuan and eighty ...

19. Clerk: *Nei1 go3 fo3 loeng5 man1 baat3.*
this set two dollar eight

This one's two yuan and eighty.

20. C#24:   *Nei1 go3 sap6 man1.*
this one ten dollar

This one's ten yuan.

21. Clerk: *Sap6 man1 laa1, sap6 ng5 man1, ni1 go3.*
ten dollar TW fifteen dollar this

Ten yuan. Fifteen yuan, this one.

22. C#24:   *Sap6 ng5.*
fifteen

Fifteen.

23. Clerk: *Gam2 m4 hai6, loeng5 man1 baat3,*
that not be two dollar eight

24.   *m4 zau6 hai2 sap6 cat1 man1 man1. Am1 m4 Am1?*
not then be seventeen dollar eight right not right

Isn't that two yuan and eighty?
Isn't it all seventeen yuan and eighty? Right?

25. C#24:   *Am1 di1 laa1.*
right little TW

Kind of right.

26. Clerk: *Am1 di1 laa1. Nei5 dai1 laa1.*
right little TW you have-a-good-deal TW

Kind of. You got a good bargain, you ...

(They go on talking)

The face strategies found in the above example focus on personal connections and rapport talk. When the chairman makes a request to get one more roll

of stamps (line 1), the clerk does not just hand him the stamps and give the price like she does with the other customers. She repeats his request (line 2) and then brags about how favorably she is treating the chairman (lines 11-14), saying that only people of her personal connections ("Going through the backdoor" is a popular expression in Chinese referring to getting things through personal connections) can have these stamps. A distinctive feature of Chinese culture is that it lays greater emphasis than other cultures on the use of personal connections. But these ties are more instrumental than personal in nature (King, 1992; Zhao & Gao, 1990). For instance, the chairman can use his *guanxi* with the clerk to get stamps that are not available to ordinary customers and, in turn, the chairman will return this favor to the clerk in one way or another. This is why establishing a personal connection is often an important move in Chinese politeness behavior.

Within this kind of inside relationship, face strategies emphasizing rapport are frequently used. For instance, the clerk asks the chairman to calculate the price to make sure that she is doing a good job—inviting the hearer to participate (lines 16-24). In the last line, the clerk is joking with the chairman ("you got a good bargain"). Their interaction does not end abruptly with the completion of the transaction. Instead, it goes on for a few more seconds with the clerk explaining when other kinds of stamps can be purchased. The fact that both the clerk and customers she is acquainted with are willing to spend time and effort on engaging in small talk is a sign of their mutual consideration of face. By talking about topics unrelated to business, they show rapport and interest in maintaining a good relationship, reframing the business transaction as a socializing event. This is quite different from the interaction with a customer the clerk does not know.

SOCIAL DISTANCE IN POLITENESS BEHAVIOR

There are two systems at work in service encounters at state-run stores, depending on the personal relationships between the clerk and the customer. When the clerk and the customer do not know each other, they only recognize the task of the encounter—to get things done. Verbal interaction is terse and carried out only to facilitate the completion of the task. Openings and closings of the interaction are rarely elaborated, and there is little use of politeness strategies. When the clerk and the customer are acquainted, their social network is recognized and emphasized, and verbal interaction becomes a process of reinforcing the social connection. This gives rise to the use of positive politeness strategies like small talk, joking, use of ingroup language, and so forth. Consequently, being acquainted with someone is a major factor in the use of politeness strategies.

This seems to confirm the general belief that there is a large gap between ingroup members and outgroup members in Chinese culture and that social distance is a prominent feature in politeness behavior. In comparing the ways Americans and Chinese deal with people in an outside relation, psychologist Michael Bond (1994) comments that while Americans take communication as a way to establish relationship, Chinese rarely communicate with people they don't know. This can lead Americans to think that Chinese are not very friendly. This is because Chinese make a clear distinction between people they know and people they don't know. Chinese mainly talk with people they know, and are not interested in talking with others. What is more, they may be very suspicious of those who initiate the conversation if unacquainted. This characteristic of Chinese communication patterns is reflected in the significantly different way the clerk interacts with customers with whom she is acquainted and those with whom she is not. In the inside relation of acquaintance, participants use more elaborated linguistic codes and face strategies to engage in conversation.

But we also need to look at the issue from a historic perspective: that is the socialist system practiced in China for nearly 50 years. It has affected politeness behavior in contemporary China in two ways. First, the state-run service business was established based on the ideology that everybody should be equal and be able to receive good service, and that practicing a socialist moral code could ensure good service. Under this system, the dominant ideological belief is that doing business, making money and serving customers are not the goal in a service encounter, while serving the country and the people is the purpose of any job. But serving the country and the people is so abstract that it remains a vague and empty political slogan in people's minds. Consequently service people are not motivated to pay attention to the interpersonal aspect of the service encounter, and politeness rituals are completely ignored.

Secondly, the practice of socialism and the political environment (particularly the Cultural Revolution) in contemporary China have elevated the importance of personal connections in social life and social interaction. Personal connections provide access to all kinds of privileges and material benefits ranging from power and high position to job assignments, housing, and daily necessities. Personal connections cannot afford to be neglected. People are very careful about how to create and maintain personal networks so that they can get better service even in an unimportant situation such as buying stamps. State power has also been undermined because of the flourishing practice of reliance on personal connections to get things done. There is no checking system in state-run stores to monitor service or to regulate professional conduct. The service person can get access to certain things that were not readily available in the market and use this as a means for building personal connections. Customers, in order to get things that they need but that are not easy to find on the market, mobilize their personal connections to obtain such things. It is thus crucial to keep a good relationship with one's acquaintances.

There are two contributing social factors to politeness behavior in Chinese service encounters. One is the Chinese cultural norm of distinction between inside and outside relationship, which keeps people from interacting with an outsider.

The other is social practice under the socialist system in state-run businesses. These two factors reduce the motivation and the need on the part of the service person to create a public image of good manners and good public relations with customers. When one factor changes, the situation is quite different. For instance, in a state-run business, if the server and the customer are acquainted, the nature of their relationship switches from an outside to an inside one. Personal connections then come into the picture and play a deciding role in politeness behavior. In the following chapter, we will notice that when the operational system of service encounters changes, politeness behavior takes a different form. That is, when private business comes into China's service industry as a result of economic reforms, it forces a change in the way language is used and the way facework is applied. So linguistic politeness is a reflection of traditional cultural values as well as current social practices. In order to thoroughly understand politeness practice in China, we need to consider it in relation to its connections with traditional culture, the development of state-socialist economy in the past 50 years and the social changes that have taken place during the reform era in the last two decades.

3

"YOU ARE MY FRIEND": BUILDING OF CONNECTION IN A BUSINESS SETTING

In the last chapter, I emphasized the importance of social distance as indicated by the distinction between inside and outside relationship in a situation in which the participants interact with each other for a temporary contact such as a service encounter. How and when facework is applied depends on the social distance between the two speakers and whether there is a pre-existing relationship. Since there is a relatively large gap between ingroup and outgroup members, Chinese people tend to socialize with ingroup members and exclude outgroup members (Bond, 1994). It is within the inside relationship that social etiquette, politeness rituals and facework are elaborated most. In an outside relationship, facework is given the least consideration or perceived as least important. Interaction with strangers in the public domain is not perceived as important in social etiquette. In service encounters where there is only a temporary outside relationship, the amount of facework is measured against the social distance in interpersonal relationship, and applied when the two participants are acquainted with each other.

This is true not only in a store where the server and the customer are engaged in a brief social interaction, but also in other institutionalized settings where service is provided, such as banks, hospitals, post offices, and hotels. In studying nurse-patient interaction in a Chinese hospital, Gu (1996a) observes that Chinese business interaction is generally cold and task-oriented. Neither the nurse nor the patient uses any face redressive devices to deal with each other. Only after some time when the nurse and the patient have developed some kind of connection do they start to interact in a more friendly and polite way. Also, good interpersonal communication skill is judged in terms of being family like, that is, warm, caring and involving. A professional way of being polite in interpersonal communication in the workplace is lacking.

Private businesses were revived in China as a result of Deng Xiaoping's economic reform and Open Door policy in the early 1980s. Under the reform policy, individual citizens were allowed to set up small businesses in the service industry to supplement the state-run service businesses. The government set restrictions and administrative regulations on the scale of private businesses and the number of people they could employ. These regulations were set to ensure that private businesses would not take over state-run businesses and result in large-scale privatization. Under this policy, private business was very much run as a family business, and was operated on a limited scale. Typical private businesses were small restaurants, convenience stores, boutiques, and repair shops. With the return of private businesses in the 1980s, the need to attract business led to a new ideology of service to customers. Interpersonal interaction became an important element in service encounters, with facework applied to ensure smooth communication and business transaction. This change in economic situation has affected the language situation in China (Zhu & Cheng, 1991). The discourse mode that has been heavily influenced by politics began to give way to a new business-oriented discourse mode. One obvious difference is how people in private businesses turn an outside relation into an inside one in order to achieve the pragmatic purpose of doing business. Facework is needed to establish the connection, which is normally the first step in doing business in the Chinese context (cf. Lewis, 1996). The employment of facework in service encounters signals a change in linguistic behavior in the public domain in the economic reform era. Gu (1996b) identifies two discourse modes in contemporary China: revolutionary discourse and reform discourse. Revolutionary discourse is associated with the Mao era (1949–1977), with heavy usage of political terms and words that suggest political struggle and proletarian ideology. With Deng Xiaoping's launch of economic reform in 1979, language use in China shows a significant change from a politicizing discourse mode into an economy-driven discourse mode. The change includes naming, address forms, and word usages that give positive value to doing business and making money. For instance, the common names for children or places in the revolutionary era were words that suggest loyalty to the party and Mao Zedong (for example, *Weihong* "to protect the red," *Weidong* "to safeguard Mao Zedong"). In the reform era, words that are associated with wealth and prosperity are favored in naming. The commonly used address form of "comrade" in the revolutionary era was replaced by "Mr." or "Miss" in the reform period (Fang & Heng, 1983; Scotton & Zhu, 1983). Even in public signs in many Chinese cities, political slogans were covered by commercial advertisements taking the form of political slogans or adopting foreign styles, which shows an ideological shift from an emphasis on politics to an appreciation of developing the economy and business (Scollon & Pan, 1997; Pan, 1999).

To a great extent, linguistic behavior in the state-run business represents the revolutionary discourse and that in the private business embodies the reform discourse. Analysis of facework in social encounters similar in nature (that is, service encounters) but with different operational and managerial systems (that is, state-run versus private business) provides a deeper understanding of the pragmatic as well as the dynamic function of politeness in institutionalized interaction. When it comes to politeness behavior in a private business service encounter, the interactional style that is found in interaction among acquaintances is adopted in an outside business relation. Participants use involvement strategies to claim connection as a way to show friendliness. In other words, people try to create an inside relationship out of a temporary contact.

In the previous chapter, I showed that in business settings, when one factor changes, for example a change in the type of social relation (outside versus inside), there is a significant difference in politeness behavior. In other words, the use of face strategies is dependent upon the type of social relation and personal connections. In this chapter, I attempt to capture the linguistic strategies used to attend to face needs by both the salesperson and the customer in the private sector where the organizational structure is different from that of a state-run business. I will argue that politeness practice is a dynamic process which reflects social change. It involves not only power relations and social distance, but also how participants interpret these relations in a changing society. The impact of the change over the last decade from a state-socialist planned economy to a free-market economy affects almost every sphere of Chinese society. Linguistic politeness as a language phenomenon embodies this change in a subtle but significant way. Before economic reform, politeness behavior in the business setting was motivated by personal connections. In the period since elements of market economy were introduced into China, the use of facework has come to be triggered by the motivation for monetary gain, and personal connection is emphasized as a means to achieve and create an inside relationship in a business setting, and is itself an end. In order to achieve this effect, linguistic politeness is applied to smooth the interaction by focusing on the interpersonal aspect of the social activity.

In this chapter, I focus on interactions in one privately owned store to illustrate how politeness is achieved in an outside relationship. The privately owned store chosen for study is a women's clothing store with one saleswoman in her 20s. It is a small shop in a big shopping mall filled with privately owned stores. One day two female customers, Lanlan and Nanying, come to the clothing store. Lanlan and Nanying are colleagues in a bank, both in their 30s. Lanlan is here to exchange a sweater she bought some days ago. Nanying has brought her two-year-old daughter. They were here to exchange the sweater five days ago, but were told to come back because the owner did not have the desired sweater in stock. In this encounter, Lanlan exchanges her sweater, and Nanying buys a sweater.

The verbal interaction is prolonged, with elaborate opening and closing remarks and heavy use of positive politeness strategies. Both the saleswoman and the customers actively participate in the verbal interaction and switch between the two language codes of Mandarin and Cantonese to accommodate each other. The saleswoman is particularly keen on giving opinions and suggestions, trying hard to persuade her customers into buying. The encounter in this privately owned store is towards the other end of the politeness scale different from the situation in the stamp store, where interactions are of a task-oriented nature. Here the effort is to build relationship and to create camaraderie with the ultimate goal of doing business. The subsequent sections of the chapter look at these features in detail.

OPENING AND CLOSING OF THE ENCOUNTER

In chapter 2 it was shown that in a state-run store, the opening of the service encounter is usually a direct request from the customer, and the server rarely acknowledges the arrival of the customer. The encounter is often terminated abruptly without much exchange of politeness rituals. In contrast, most service people in privately owned stores take the initiative in greeting their customers and offering service by saying: *"Jiu1 di1 mat1je5?"* (What would you like?) or *"Jiu1 tai2 di1 mat1je5?"* (What would you like to look at?). Often there is a certain amount of chatting in the interaction that creates a friendly atmosphere. For example, in this women's clothing store, the opening and closing of the encounter are filled with phatic talk and linguistic politeness.

> ***Example 3.1.*** Lanlan comes to the store to get a sweater. She was in the store five days ago to return a sweater she had bought.

    1. SW: *Ai, gam1 ci4 gaa3?*
               Hi so late TW

               Hi, why so late?

    2. Lanlan: *Aa1, sap6baat3 hou6. Gai3 zeng3 nei1go3 si4 gaan3.*
               ah, eighteen number count right this time

    3.   *Nei5 waa6 ng5 jat6 si4 gaan3 gaa1 maa3.*
               you say five days time GW TW

Oh, it's the 18th. You said it would be five days and I planned on it.

4. SW: *Bat1 gwo3 ngo5 lau4 zo2 bei2 nei5.*
             but I save GW for you

             But I've saved it for you.

5. Lanlan: *Lau4 zo2 mei6 aa1?*
             save GW not QW

             Have you?

6. SW: *Nei5 hai6 m4 hai6 jiu1 luk6 sik1?*
             you be not be want green color

             Is it true that you want the green?

7. Lanlan: *Hai6 aa1, nei5 lo2 jat1 gin6 luk6 sik1 tai2 haa5*
             Yes TW you get one MW green color look MW

             Yes. Can you get me a green one to look at?

8. SW: *Hung4 sik1 jik6 hou2 hou2 sik1.*
             red color also very nice color

             The red color is also very pretty.

9. Lanlan: *Nei5 go2 gin6 maai6 zo2 ceot1 heoi3 mei6?*
             you that MW sell GW out not

             Did you sell that one? (referring to the sweater she returned)

10. SW: *Maai6 zo2. Go2 gin6 dai6 yi6 jat6 zo2 maai6 zo2 laa1.*
             sell GW that MW second day then sell GW TW

             Yes, that one was sold the day after you were here.

11. Lanlan: *Ou3, gam2 zau6 hou2.*
             oh that then good

             Oh, that's good then.

             (The saleswoman gets the green sweater out from under the counter)

In this encounter the saleswoman is the one that greets the customers and opens the interaction. Instead of a ceremonial greeting of "Hello, how are you?" her greeting is an utterance that shows her recognition of the customer who bought a sweater from her a few days ago ("Hi, why so late?" line 1). The utterance is said with a softening tone (indicated by the tone word *gaa*) and without address form or formulaic expression, which is just the way a person greets his/her old friend in Chinese (see also Example 2.10 in chapter 2 where the clerk in the stamp store greets a customer she knows with a "hi"). Then the saleswoman assures Lanlan that she has saved the green sweater for her (line 4). This immediate recognition and assurance from the saleswoman gives a personal feeling. The customer is also actively engaged in the conversation by telling the saleswoman why she has come on this particular day (line 2–3). Lanlan wants to look at the sweater she has in mind (a green one), but she does not make her request until the saleswoman confirms her color choice (line 6). When Lanlan makes a request (line 7), the saleswoman does something more than merely complying with what is being requested—she makes another offer by saying that the red color is also very pretty (line 8). Then they talk about the sweater that Lanlan returned earlier (lines 9–11). It is only after several turn exchanges that the saleswoman gets to the act—showing Lanlan the green sweater.

In this interaction, the introduction of the topic is delayed until after a period of facework, which is indicated by the engagement in friendly chat by the saleswoman and the customer. By spending time chatting, both the saleswoman and customer show face concern to each other and create a friendly atmosphere for the business transaction. It does not sound like an abrupt business encounter, but rather like a casual chat between friends.

The closing of the encounter is also elaborated with many politeness strategies attending to the positive face of the customer.

> ***Example 3.2.***   The two customers, Lanlan and Nanying, have completed their purchases
>
> 1. SW: (To Lanlan) *M4 goi1 nei5 wo3.*
>   thank you TW
>
> 2.   (To Nanying) *Naa4, ou3, do1 ze6 wo3.*
>   there oh, many thanks TW
>
>   (To Lanlan) Thank you.
>   (To Nanying) Here you are. Thanks a lot.
>
> 3. Daughter: *Do1 ze6.*
>   many thanks
>
>   Thanks a lot.
>
> 4. SW: *Haa1, gam3 lek1, nei5 go3 neoi5.*
>   (laugh) so smart your daughter
>
>   (laugh) Oh, your daughter is so smart.
>
> 5. Nanying: (laugh)

(SW and Nanying keep talking about the little girl for a few exchanges)

6. SW: *ji5 hau6 lai4 gwo3 laa1, hou2 maa1?*
later come again TW OK TW

Come back some other time, Okay?

7. Lanlan: *Hou2 aa1, ji5 hau6.*
OK TW later

Okay, some other time.

8. SW: *Ci4 di1 jau5 gei1 wui6, tai2 zung3 nei1 zau6*
later have chance look like GW then

9. *bong1 can3 laa1.*
come-buy TW

Later when (you) have a chance, when (you) see something you like, just come and buy it.

10. Lanlan: *Hou2 waa1, hou2 waa1.*
OK TW OK TW

Okay, Okay.

(Lanlan and Nanying leave the store)

In contrast to the encounters in the stamp store where no verbal expression of the closing is uttered, in this privately owned store the closing of the interaction is fully expressed linguistically. First there are pre-closing remarks by the saleswoman (lines 1–2) to thank both her customers. Then the saleswoman compliments the little girl (line 4) and starts talking about the little girl with Nanying as a way to be friendly. As Wolfson (1983) notes, compliments attend to the positive face of the hearer and have the function of maintaining a social relationship. The saleswoman is using a positive politeness strategy. She continues, exchanging a few turns with Nanying about the little girl. And then she invites them to come to the store again for future business (line 6). In Chinese, it is a common practice to give an invitation as a closing remark. An invitation is intrinsically polite in that it shows the current speaker's wish to do something nice for the hearer.

So the closing of the encounter consists of four parts: thanking, complimenting, inviting, and final closing. Each part has a pragmatic function. The thanking part serves the function of pre-closing for a smooth business transaction. The complimenting part reinforces the established relationship between the server and the customer. The invitation projects a future business relationship. And then the final closing of the customer accepting the invitation embodies a polite way to end the encounter. Of course, not every encounter in a privately owned store necessarily consists of these four parts. This is a typical example to show how the closing is done through elaborate facework. But in most cases salespeople in privately owned stores employ one, two, or all of these face strategies to close an encounter and foster better business relationships and chances for future business.

CODE-SWITCHING AS A FACE STRATEGY

As explained earlier, code-switching is the use of more than one language in the course of a single speech event, or going from one language to the other in midspeech when both speakers know the two languages (Saville-Troike, 1989). There is much speculation explaining why a speaker alternates between language codes. Blom and Gumperz (1972) distinguish two kinds of code-switching: situational code-switching and metaphorical code-switching. Situational code-switching occurs when there is a change in the topic or participants, while metaphorical code-switching signals a change in role-relationship such as group membership and ingroup/outgroup distinction. Gumperz (1982) also identifies code-switching as a conversational strategy that is associated with social identity. Giles's (Giles et al., 1913; Giles, 1977) accommodation theory establishes the link between language choice and the social status of the speaker. The speaker can alternate language codes to show convergence or divergence with the hearer depending on how the social relation is viewed, for example, dominant group versus subordinate group. Code-switching is thus an index of social relations.

China is a multilingual society with eight mutually unintelligible spoken languages sharing one writing system (DeFrancis, 1984). Many linguists have acknowledged the complexity of China's language situation and the hostilities it creates among speakers of different dialects in China (for example, DeFrancis, 1984; Erbaugh, 1995). Although Mandarin or what is called *Putonghua* (common language) in China has been the national standard language in Mainland China since the mid–1950s, only a small number of dialect-speaking people are true bilinguals in Mandarin and their local dialects. This is particularly true in Guangzhou, a Cantonese-speaking area. In terms of phonological, lexical and syntactic features, Mandarin and Cantonese are as different as the two languages of German and English.

Prior to the economic reform in the early 1980s, in spite of the Chinese government's efforts to promote the use of Mandarin as part of the language reform campaign,[8] Mandarin Chinese was used in quite limited domains and spoken with a variety of local accents. The locals in Guangdong Province, although they can understand Mandarin, speak only Cantonese in almost all domains, including government administration, public services, service encounters, at home, and on school playgrounds as well as in classrooms where subjects other than Chinese are taught. In other words, Cantonese is the language of daily life in the Cantonese-speaking region. Mandarin speakers often encounter difficulties in communicating with service people in Guangdong and complain about the unfriendliness and even hostility they encounter in the service industry, because service people simply ignore Mandarin-speaking customers. Because of this, Guangzhou service people are notorious for their *"pai wai"* (excluding outsiders) attitude. Economic reform in the 1980s brought about some changes in the structure of the service industry (with the boom in privately owned shops) as well as the attitude of the service people. In previous studies (Pan, 1997b, in press a, in press b) I found that while service people in state-run businesses do not switch from Cantonese to Mandarin to accommodate Mandarin-speaking customers, salespeople in private business have made an effort to speak Mandarin in spite of their low proficiency level in the language. Code-switching has thus become a sign of their friendliness and a means for salespeople to interact with the customer.

In the privately owned women's clothing store under study, the two female customers are bilingual in Mandarin and Cantonese. The saleswoman is a native speaker of Cantonese and also speaks some Mandarin. Unlike the situation in a state-run store where code-switching rarely occurs, in this privately owned store both the customers and the saleswoman switch between Mandarin and Cantonese to conduct business. There is a mutual cooperation in language choice that makes the conversation smooth and friendly. The following excerpt exemplifies code-switching employed by the customer and the saleswoman:

Example 3.3.   When Lanlan asks Nanying's opinion on the sweater

    1. Lanlan: (Mandarin, to Nanying)
                   Ni3 shuo1 zhe4 ge hao3 bu4 hao3?
                   you say this good no good

    2.   *Zhe4 ge jiao4 shenme xian4 zai rong2,*
                   this MW call what thread wool

    3.   *jiu4 shuo1 zen3 me xi3 ah dou1 bu4 bian4 xing2.*
                   just say how wash TW still not change shape

                   What do you think of this? This is called knitting wool. They say that no matter how you wash it, it won't change its shape.

    4. SW: (Mandarin)
                   Ai4, zhe4 ge liang4.
                   yeah, this MW pretty

    5.   (Cantonese)
                   Sai2 gei2 nin4 dou1 gam3 leng3 gaa3
                   wash few year still so pretty TW

    6.   *Jan4 dei6 zoek3 zo2 nei1 go3 liu6 aa1,*
                   people wear GW this MW material TW

    7.   *nin4 nin4 dou1 hing1 gaa3.*
                   year year still fashion TW

    8.   *Bat1gwo3 go2di1 faa1 sik1 m4 tung4 zi1maa3.*
                   But those collor pattern not same TW

9.   *Gau6 nin4 nei1 ni1dou6 jat1 lap1 lap1 zan1 zyu1.*
            last year TW here one MW MW pearl

10.   *Go2 go2 maai6 jat1 baak3, gau2sap6.*
            that MW sell one hundred ninety

            (Mandarin) Right, this is pretty.
            (Cantonese) It stays in good shape even after years of washing.
            Everyone wears this kind of material.
            It has been in fashion for years.
            The only difference is the style.
            In last year's style, there were pearls dotted here (on the
            sweater).
            That one sold for a hundred, or ninety (dollars).

11. Lanlan: (Cantonese)
            Ngo5 zau6 hai6 m4 zung1ji3 gam3 do1
            I just be not like so much

12.   *zan1zyu1i. Gam3 joeng6 gaan2gaan2daan1daan1.*
            pearl such way simple-simple

            I just don't like so many pearls. I prefer the simple style like
            this.

13. SW: (Cantonese)
            Go2di1 fing6 loeng5 fing6 zau6 lat1 laa1.
            those shake two shake then loose GW

14.   *Nei1di1 fing6 gik6 dou1 m4 bin3.*
            these shake hard still not change.

            Those (pearls) will get loose if you shake the sweater.
            But this one will keep its shape no matter how hard you shake it.

In the above example, Lanlan asks Nanying's opinion on the sweater in Mandarin (line 1). She uses Mandarin as their ingroup dialect, as the two are accustomed to speaking Mandarin to each other. But when Lanlan talks to the saleswoman in line 11, she uses Cantonese. This is an example of situational code-switching. That is, the switch shows a change in setting and a change in addressee; she uses Mandarin for friends' talk and Cantonese for business talk.

As for the saleswoman, she follows the customers' language choice; when the customers talk in Mandarin, she uses Mandarin (line 4); when they talk in Cantonese, she switches to Cantonese (line 13). She alternates between the two codes to render her support in the dialect choice as a way of showing her willingness to accommodate her customers. She first gets the floor by offering her opinion in Mandarin (line 4). It is not her native language, but she uses it to claim common ground with the customers. After getting the floor, she switches to Cantonese to elaborate her point (line 5), since it is easier for her to make her argument in her native dialect. This code-switching indicates a shift of footing (Goffman's term, 1974, 1981); she first uses Mandarin to identify herself as belonging to the same group as the customers and gain their trust. She then shifts her footing to that of a saleswoman by using Cantonese, because she is a better salesperson when speaking Cantonese and it serves her self-interest to make money. Here the linguistic choice becomes a symbol or metaphor for the relationship being enacted; Mandarin is chosen for enhancing personal relationships, whereas Cantonese symbolizes her position as a saleswoman. The alternation between the two languages facilitates the interaction between the customer and the server. The conversation thus flows easily without any language problems.

RENDERING OPINIONS AND SUGGESTIONS

Compared to the terse, brief exchange between the clerk and her customers in the state-run stamp store, the interaction in the privately owned clothing store is much longer, filled with exchanges of utterances between the saleswoman and the two customers. All three parties actively participate in the transaction, engaging themselves in an interaction that goes beyond a one-time business transaction. This active participation creates an atmosphere of friendliness and politeness. The saleswoman is particularly eager to render her opinions and make suggestions so as to reassure her customers of a good choice of merchandise as shown in Example 3.4.

Example 3.4.   Lanlan is returning a sweater for exchange, and the saleswoman is showing her a new one

1. SW: *Nei1 di1 leng3 gwo1 soeng6 ci3 laa1.*
these pretty than last time TW

These are prettier than the one you bought last time.

2. Lanlan: *Leng3 gwo1 soeng6 ci3.*
pretty than last time

Prettier than the last one.

3. SW: *Go2 gin6 maai6 zo2 laa1, jau6.*
that MW sell GW TW too

That one is sold out, too.

4. Lanlan: *Maai6 zo2 laa1. Gam2 zau6 hou2 aa1.*
sell GW TW so just good TW

Sold out? That's good.

5. SW: *So2ji5 ngo5 dou1 giu3 nei5 fong3 dai1. Zaan6 do1 di1 laa1.*
         so I also ask you leave down earn more some TW

         That's why I asked you to leave it here. Earn more money.

6. Lanlan: *Daai6gaa1 fun1hei2.*
            everyone happy

7.   *Hai6 nei5 jau6 gou1hing3, ngo5 jau6 gou1hing3.*
         be you too glad I too glad

         Everybody is happy then.
         You're happy, and I'm happy, too.

8. SW: *Hai6 aa1. Ngo5 waa6, ngo5 jing1sing4 dak1 nei5,*
         be TW I say I promise can you

9.   *ngo5 bong1 nei5 lo2 faan1 gin6 leng3 ge3.*
         I help you get back MW pretty TW

         That's right. As I said, I promised,
         that I would get you a nicer one.

10. Lanlan: *Hai6, hai6.*
             be be

             Yes, yes.

11. SW: *Nei5 fong3sam1 laa1.*
          you at-ease TW

12.   *So2ji5 ngo5 gong2 dak1 dou3 zou6 dak1 dou3*
          so I say can GW do can GW

          Don't you worry.
          I always keep my word.

Upon showing the new sweater, the saleswoman, instead of asking the customer's opinion, makes the first comment (line 1), an affirmative statement that this sweater is prettier than the last one. She is assuming that "I believe this is what you want, and I do it for you," a strategy addressing the positive face of the hearer. Her promises in lines 8-9 and 11-12 add to this effect. As Brown and Levinson put it, a promise is a way of showing the speaker's cooperation with the hearer. It demonstrates the speaker's good intention in satisfying the hearer's positive face wants (1987, p. 125). Therefore, the use of this positive politeness strategy by the saleswoman stresses her intention to be helpful to the customers. Lanlan is responding to the saleswoman's remark about selling the sweater by giving expression to the feelings of both of them (line 6, "Everyone is happy then. You're happy, and I'm happy, too"). This mutual emphasis on the positive face need of the other keeps the interaction going like a conversation between two friends.

The following sequence is another example of how the saleswoman is involved in the interaction.

Example 3.5.   Nanying is looking at a sweater

    1. SW: (Cantonese)
Ni1 go3 sik1 leng3 di1 aa1.
this color pretty more TW

    2.   *Can3 haak1 sik1 jau6 leng3.*
match black color also pretty

    3.   *Dak6 ji3 wan2 dou1 wan2 go2 dou6 aa1.*
specially find also find there TW

    4.   *Siu2 gei2 man1 ngo5 dou1 lo2 go2 dou6.*
less few dollar I still get there

    5.   *Jau5 di1 sik1seoi2 peng4 di1 ngo5 dou1 m4 lo2.*
some color cheap more I still not get

           This color is pretty.
It goes well with black, too.
I made a special trip there to look for the color.
Even if I make a few dollars less,
I would still get this color there.
Some colors are cheap, but I still won't get them.

    6. Nanying: (Mandarin, to Lanlan)
Mh, ni3 jue2de ta1 zhe4 li3 hen3 kuang1 ah
TW, you feel it here very loose TW

    7.   *Wai4, ni3 gen1 wo3 liang2 yi liang2 zhe4 li3.*
hi you for me measure once measure here

           Do you think it's loose here?
Hey, measure it for me here.

    8. SW: (Cantonese)
Peng4 gik6,
cheap extreme

    9.   *peng4 loeng5 saam1 man1 ngo5 dou1 m4 lo2.*
cheap two three dollar I still not take

    10.   *Zan1 hai6 gaa3,*
really be TW

    11.   *jau5 go3 dei6 fong1 peng4 loeng5 saam1 man1*
have MW place cheap two three dollar

12. *ngo5 dou1 m4 lo2.*
  I still not take

  No matter how cheap they are,
  even if they are two or three dollars less, I wouldn't take them.
  Really,
  there is a place where I can get them two or three dollars cheaper,
  but I just wouldn't take them.

13. Nanying:(Mandarin, to Lanlan)
  You3 dian3 duan3.
  have little short

  It's a bit short.

14. SW: (Cantonese)
  M4 hai6. Jat1 joeng6 ze1.
  not be same TW

15. *Nei5 gam2 joeng6, nei5 heoi3, nei5 m4 hou2 caak3,*
  you this-way you go you no good take-apart

16. *nei5 fong3 hoi1, taan1ping4, nei5.*
  you let-go lay flat you

17. *Zau6 dak1 jat1 gin6,*
  only have one MW

18. *wong4 sik1, dou1 lo2 zo2 soeng5 lai4.*
  yellow color all take GW up come

  No, it's the same.
  You, this way … you go to … don't take it apart.
  You just let go of it and lay it flat, you …
  This is the only one.
  The yellow ones are all here.

19. Lanlan: (Mandarin, to Nanying)
  Zhe4 yang4, wo3 zhe4 ge4, ba3 zhei4 ge4 …
  this way I this take this

  This way, I, this, take this …

20. Nanying:(Mandarin, to Lanlan)
  Zhei4 ling3 shi4 kuan1 yi1dian3 ah, zhei4 ge4
  this collar be loose a little TW this one

  The collar is a bit loose, this …

21. Nanying:(Cantonese, to SW)
  M4 hai6, nei1go3,
  not be this MW

22.	*wai3, nei1 go3 hou2 ci5 hai6 fut3 di1, hai6 m4 hai6?*
	hi this seem be wide bit be not be

	No, this.
	Hey, this is a bit loose, right?

23. SW:	(Cantonese)
	Bin1 go3?
	Which one

	Which one?

24. Lanlan:	(Mandarin)
	Yi1 jia4 nong4 de, ke3neng2
	hanger cause GW maybe

	Perhaps it's caused by hanging on the hanger.

25. Nanying:(Mandarin)
	Shi4
	right

	Right.

26. SW:	(Cantonese)
	Go2 go3 ji1 gaa3 gwaa3 ge3, bin1 dou6 fut3 aa1.
	That one hanger hang TW where loose GW

	It's caused by hanging on the hanger. It isn't too wide.

27. Lanlan:	(Cantonese)
	Tai2 hou2 lai1
	look carefully come

28.	(Mandarin)
	yao4 bu4 ran2 you4 de2 zou3 yi1 ci4 ma2 fan2 le
	otherwise again must come one time trouble GW

	(Cantonese) Take a careful look at it,
	(Mandarin) otherwise you have to come again.
	That will be a lot of trouble.

29. SW:	(Cantonese)
	Nei5 zoek3 jat1 haa5.
	You wear once

	You try it on.

In this segment, two interactions are going on concurrently; Nanying is talking to Lanlan while the saleswoman is talking to both of them. Nanying is looking at a sweater and the saleswoman is trying to talk her into buying it. The two interactions overlap, and the saleswoman's utterances are much longer. She first makes a comment on the color of the sweater, suggesting that it would go well with black (lines 1-2). Then from lines 3 to 5 and lines 8 to 12 she tells the story of how she made a special effort in order to get this stock for the store (privately owned clothing stores have to get their stock from Hong Kong). In fact, how she got the stock has little to do with how pretty the color of the sweater is. She is giving irrelevant information here, which is a violation of the Gricean maxim of relevance (Grice, 1975). But the underlying notion is to draw attention from the customers, who are talking between themselves, as if she were saying: "Look, I made a special effort to get this color. And you should appreciate it." When Nanying says that the sweater is too short, the saleswoman carefully shows Nanying how to measure it (lines 14–18) and suggests that Nanying try it on.

Rendering opinions, giving suggestions, and telling narratives are features that express the speaker's high involvement in the interaction, which creates the stylistic effect of rapport (Tannen, 1986). In the above example, the saleswoman keeps providing opinions and suggestions as a way to show her involvement with the customer. Of course, her real intention is to get the customer to buy the merchandise. But by getting closer to the customer, the saleswoman makes it sound like a personal favor to provide the merchandise and that there is an obligation on the part of the customer to buy it.

CLAIM OF CONNECTION

Connection building as a business strategy is practiced in many Asian cultures. For example, in Japanese business settings, building a trustworthy relationship is the first step in conducting business, which is different from the American practice of "business is business" (Nakano, 1995; Yamada, 1992). In a culture that emphasizes group cohesion and the interdependence among group members, claim of connection is the first entry into a group and establishing an in-group identity. Thus it serves two functions: to create an identity in the participation framework (Goffman's term, 1981) so that the speaker and the hearer can relate to each other, and to attend to face need by shortening the distance between interlocutors.

This is exactly the strategy the saleswoman in the clothing store uses to close the business deal. Lanlan has exchanged the sweater she bought a few days ago and is looking at a blouse. Nanying is looking at another sweater and is undecided about whether to buy it. The saleswoman emphasizes the aspect of personal connection as a technique to persuade Nanying to buy the sweater.

> ***Example 3.6.***   Lanlan has bought a sweater, and Nanying is looking at a
> sweater of similar style. Nanying is not sure whether to
> buy or not. The saleswoman starts to talk

1. SW: [Cantonese]
    Ngo5 lam2 zyu6 zau6hai6 nei5dei6 gam2 mat1je5,
    I think GW just you-plural so what

2.   *zau6 hai6 suk6 ngo5.*
    just be familiar me

3.   *Peng4 di1 bei2 nei5dei6.*
    cheap little give you-plural

4.   *Zau6hai6 gong1gong1 maai6 baat3sap6 ng5 man1.*
    just be just-now sell eighty five dollar

    I'm just thinking that you are so …
    That's, know me well.
    I'll give you a discount.
    Even just now I sold it for eighty-five dollars.

5. Nanying: (Mandarin, to Lanlan)
    Zhe4 shi4 wo3 de.
    this be mine

    This is mine.

6. SW: (Cantonese)
    Zau6 hai6 ngo5 lam2 zyu6 nei5 dei6
    just be I think GW you-plural

7.   *dai6 gaa1 gam3 lou5 jau5, m4 gaai3ji3*
    everyone so old friend not mind

8.   *faan2zeng3 ngo5 dou1 ji4gaa1, mat1je5,*
    anyway I also now what

9.   *peng4 loeng5 man1 bei2 nei5*
    cheap two dollar give you

    Just because I think you,
    You are all my friends, I don't mind …
    Anyway, I, also, now … what,
    Give you two dollars discount.

10. Lanlan: (Cantonese)
    Bei2 ngo5 tai2 go2 gin6 can3ji1 aa1
    give me look that MW blouse TW

    Show me that blouse.

11. SW: (Cantonese)
    Hou2 waa1
    good TW

Okay.

12. Nanying: (Mandarin, to Lanlan)
Yao4 bu1 yao4?
want not want

Should I buy it or not?

13. SW: (Cantonese)
Syun3 laak3, bei2 maai4 nei5 laa1.
not-mind TW give also you TW

14.   *Hai2 aa1, zan1 hai6 tai2 hai2 aa3 sou2 fan6 soeng6.*
Be TW really be see at sister-in-law face on

OK, I'll give you a discount too.
Really, I'm doing this just as a favor for this sister.

15. Lanlan: *Tai2 aa3 sou2 fan6 aa1, jau6 peng4 bei2 nei5 aa1.*
see sister-in-law face TW also cheap give you TW

She's doing me a favor, and she's giving you a discount, too.

16. Nanying:*Jau6 peng4.*
also cheap

Give me a discount, too.

17. Lanlan: *Gei2 zin2 aa1?*
how-much money TW

How much?

18. SW: *Cat1 sap6 ng5.*
seventy five

Seventy-five yuan.

19. Lanlan: *Cat1 sap6 ng5.*
Seventy five

Seventy-five yuan.

20. SW: *Syun3 laak3.*
never-mind TW

21.   *Aa1, faan2 zeng3 ngo5 dou1 dong3 do1 jyu4 gaa3 laa1,*
TW anyway I just consider surplus GW TW

22.   *dong3 nei5 dei6 ...*
consider you-plural

> Never mind.
> Ah, anyway I'm not counting this one.
> Just take you as ...
>
> (Nanying takes out money)

There are two techniques that the saleswoman uses here to claim the connection. One is explicitly making the connection that the customers are her friends ("I'm just thinking that you are so ... know me well." lines 1–2) and using a kinship term *aa-sou* (sister-in-law) to refer to Lanlan ("Really, I'm doing this just as a favor for this sister." line 14). The factor of ingroup identity plays a crucial role here. Originally there is only a temporary outside relationship of service business between the saleswoman and her customers. But the saleswoman resorts to the claim of connection in order to create an ingroup relationship with her customers, for "friend" in the Chinese context carries the connotation of mutual responsibility and mutual dependency. And the extended use of kinship terms as address forms enhances the closeness of the relation. She uses a linguistic strategy to create an inside relationship with her customers.

The other technique is to emphasize closeness with the customers. The saleswoman repeatedly says that the customers know her so well and that she is giving Nanying a discount as a favor for Lanlan ("OK, I'll give you a discount, too. Really, I'm doing this just as a favor for this sister," lines 13–14). In the Chinese context, the phrase "do something as a favor for somebody," which literally means "considering his/her face" (for example, in the above encounter "*Tai2 hai2 aa3 sou2 fan6 soeng6*"—considering this sister-in-law's face) is an important concept in politeness behavior. By using this phrase, the speaker indicates that the person being referred to has an important status in the speaker's mind, and that special consideration is being given to the person concerned. In this way, the saleswoman builds a base for the customers to trust her: since we are friends, I'm doing you a favor (by giving you a two dollar discount), and you have got to believe me, accept my favor and do me one in return (by buying my merchandise). And Lanlan does return "face" to the saleswoman by indirectly persuading Nanying to buy the blouse (line 15, "She's doing me a favor, and she's giving you a discount, too"). Lanlan's stance of returning "face" can also be seen in her initiative in asking the price for Nanying (line 17, "How much?").

The fact that the saleswoman succeeds in persuading her customer by claiming personal connection implies something deeper. First, personal connection suggests some obligation of both parties to take into consideration the relationship between them by acting in a way appropriate to the connection. Secondly, it has to do with the reciprocal aspect of face giving. The speaker gives face to the hearer, and the hearer returns face to the speaker. Each party takes some action to enhance the face need of the other, and in return retain or gain face for herself. This mutuality in face giving is essential in understanding Chinese politeness behavior. Without the reciprocation of face, personal connection would not go any further. But the reciprocation of face depends on the participants' role in a system that can be interpreted and understood in terms of power structure and hierarchy. That is why face is of primary concern in an inside relationship. When the clerk in the state-run store interacts with customers unacquainted with her, there is no mutual consideration of face because they do not see themselves as part of a system which relates them to each other. But the interaction is very different when the clerk sees customers she knows. In the privately owned store, the relationship between the saleswoman and the customer is at first an outside one. But through the intensive use of face strategies, the nature of their relation undergoes some change. The emphasis laid upon closeness and connectedness makes it feel like an inside relationship in which the saleswoman and the customer share the obligation of mutual face giving. Under this obligation, each party will make some compromises and make sure not to hurt the other's face by holding too strictly to one's principle. This is how facework functions in a business deal: first, build a relation that obliges both parties to grant each other's face need, then proceed to business.

Another point worth mentioning is that politeness markers play only a small part in Chinese politeness even in an inside situation. Most of the speech acts in my service encounter data are issued without politeness markers. That is to say, politeness is not so much indicated by specific linguistic features that modify the imposition of a speech act, as it is manifested through exchanges of interaction and the ways that interlocutors show involvement with each other in the interaction. For instance, the saleswoman in this privately owned store employs a variety of discursive strategies such as code-switching, rendering opinions, use of kinship terms, and claim of connection to show her friendliness and politeness to the customer.

POLITENESS BEHAVIOR IN TRANSITIONAL CHINA

From the above analysis, we can conclude that the main facework strategies employed in a Chinese service encounter are linguistic features that show the speakers' efforts to, and emphasis on building relationship. A more friendly interaction is characterized by the following features: (1) an opening initiated by the server; (2) a linguistically expressed closing; (3) a prolonged interaction filled with detailed explanations, suggestions and assurances; (4) a period of engaging in small talk; and (5) an emphasis on interpersonal relationship. These features fall into the category of positive politeness in Brown and Levinson's model and have a focus on reinforcement of an existing inside relationship. In the state-run stamp store, these features are absent in the interactions between the clerk and customers she doesn't know, while the interactions between the clerk and customers she is acquainted with possess most of these features. This exemplifies that an inside relation requires facework because of the interdependence among group members in Chinese culture.

In a privately owned store, these strategies are constantly used to turn an outside relationship into an inside one in order to ensure a smooth business transaction. Motivated by profit-making, the server in the privately owned store works to establish a personal relationship with the customer. Once this relationship is established, it is easy to carry out business and make further business deals. It can be concluded that in most cases the use of facework in service encounters is motivated by either a pre-existing personal connection, that is, an inside relationship, or by the prospect of monetary reward.

Historically, Chinese society functioned on the basis of family and clan (Shi, 1997). People outside the clan were considered rivals or enemies. An old saying in Chinese, "nei wai you bie" (inside and outside should be different), encapsulates the tendency of Chinese to treat people differently depending on whether they are in an inside or an outside relation. Even though traditional Chinese society laid great emphasis on etiquette and deference, the practice of polite behavior or being nice to others did not extend outside of the group. People are related by their ingroup identity: if you are one of us, we trust you and treat you well. If not, it doesn't matter how you are treated. The first step to enabling a smooth business transaction is to reveal an ingroup identity (if there is any) or to create an inside relation (if there is no ingroup relation). Once this relationship is established, it is easier to do business.

Before the 1949 Revolution, Chinese service businesses were mainly small family-run businesses serving local communities. Service people and customers were either neighbors or familiar acquaintances. To a large extent, they belonged to the same community and shared an ingroup identity. So politeness came to be expressed through family-like linguistic strategies such as the use of extended kinship terms and involvement strategies. After the 1949 Revolution, small family stores were turned into either state-run or collective businesses. The traditional close feeling between the store-owner and the customer became irrelevant to the new business context. Gradually the service encounter came to be perceived as a task-oriented business deal, and language use was limited to that necessary to the commercial transaction without any consideration for face concern.

As China expands its economic contact with the world, it also expands its language contact, especially in the business sector and in the public domain. The cold impersonal interaction in service encounters became a smudge on China's public image in the eyes of ever-increasing numbers of foreign tourists and business people entering China with the implementation of the Open Door policy in the early 1980s. How to improve service in service industries was the subject of many newspaper articles. Newspaper editorials, which functioned as the channel for publicizing the government's policies in socialist China, carried lengthy discussions on how to improve the situation, citing criticisms from foreign visitors. The Chinese government launched a massive campaign in the 1980s to raise the general public's awareness of language use and politeness behavior with the aim to improve society. The campaign was called Five Stresses and Four Points of Beauty (*wu jiang si mei*). The five stresses were stress on decorum, stress on manners, stress on hygiene, stress on discipline, and stress on morals (*jiang wenming, jiang limao, jiang weisheng, jiang zhixu, jiang daode*). The four points of beauty were beautification of the mind, beautification of language, beautification of behavior, and beautification of the environment (*xinling mei, yuyan mei, xingwei mei, huanjing mei*). This campaign called for public attention to proper public behavior and appropriate use of language. Big posters were put up in public places promoting the use of a set of polite expressions such as "Hello" (*nin hao*), "I'm sorry" (*duibuqi*), and "Thank you" (*xiexie*). These very basic expressions had almost entirely fallen out of use in the public domain, particularly during the Cultural Revolution when social order was completely destroyed. As a result, the basic social rules of demeanor and proper behavior had to be restored through a nationwide campaign enforced by the government administrative measures.

Because many privately owned stores are family business, the economic revival in China also saw the revival of the traditional way of being polite in the public domain including business transactions, particularly in the early stage of economic reforms. The traditional way of doing business and being polite has its roots in values of personal connection and group cohesion. The face strategies employed by the saleswoman in the women's clothing store have this feature. She uses linguistic strategies that emphasize the positive face want and closeness between the participants. The excessive use of positive politeness may sound pushy, not leaving the hearer any room to maneuver, but on the other hand it shows the cultural value of favoring connectedness.

Another trend in politeness behavior is the influence from western cultures and the adoption of polite expressions from foreign languages. During the economic reform era, many Chinese department stores and hotels were set up with foreign investment or as joint ventures. Chinese staff members went through the professional training offered by foreign companies. Public relations then became an important issue. Chinese staff members learned a set of formulaic polite expressions such as "Hello" (*nin hao*), "Welcome" (*huanying*), "Do you need help?" (*nin xuyao bangmang ma*), "Thank you for coming" (*xiexie guanglin*). These expressions cover the opening, transaction, and closing phases of a service encounter, and there is a certain element of being professionally polite in that these are formulaic and standardized expressions. If the traditional way of being polite puts emphasis on closeness and inside relations, the professional way of being polite introduces a form of distant politeness, that is, offering help and attending to face need without being too involved.

A typical example can be found in Hong Kong-owned stores in Guangzhou and Foshang, for example, Bossini, G2000, U2, and Theme. Due to its proximity to Hong Kong, Guangdong Province is heavily influenced by Hong Kong in terms of business style and language use. In the Hong Kong-owned stores, the salespersons are not allowed to sit behind the counter. They walk around the store and are trained to greet customers as they enter the store with a set phrase: "Can I help you?" (*jau5 mat1je5 bong1 dou3 nei5?*), or "Please take a look as you like" (*ceoi4bin6 tai2tai2*). The phrase *jau5 mat1je5 bong1 dou3 nei5?* is a direct translation from the English "Can I help you?" commonly used in service encounters in English-speaking cultures. This phrase is commonly used in Hong Kong, a British colony for the 150 years up to 1997. The phrase has now entered the Mainland's service industry. When a customer leaves the store, the salesperson says "Thank you" and/or "Please come again" as a closing remark. These formulaic politeness phrases give customers a warm but professional feeling. The salesperson does not actively engage in small talk with the customer or seek personal details from her to show politeness, but he/she relies more on these formulaic expressions to show professional warmth and politeness.

This change, however, may not be nationwide. In other cities of China such as Beijing, Nanjing, and Kunming, many service encounters maintain the interaction style of either being impersonal and task-oriented as in state-run businesses or being very personal as in private businesses. That is, the distinction between inside and outside relations plays a key role in the choice of linguistic politeness. The use of professional formulaic expressions is very limited, found mainly in joint-venture stores and large hotels catering to foreign travellers.

My purpose here is not to pinpoint which style is preferred in what place, but rather to make the argument that politeness behavior is so deeply engrained in social life and so much influenced by societal changes that it is almost impossible to study politeness per se without analyzing the social forces behind it. Politeness practice is a reflection of historic and social developments in a society. For example, we all agree that power relations are an important sociological variable in politeness behavior. In service encounters, the power relation between service people and customers should theoretically be constant across settings because the social roles of salespersons and customers remain the same across settings, and customers are supposed to possess purchasing power. But this very power relation can be changed if social conditions under which the interaction takes place have changed. As we have seen in these two chapters, the power relation is different in a state-run store and a privately owned store. In the state-run stamp store, the clerk is the one who has power, contrary to the common assumption that the customer holds the power because he/she possesses the money to make a purchase. Because of the institutionalized power and scarcity of merchandise in state-run businesses, typical products of a socialist planned economy, the clerk does not have to make any effort to attract customers and there is no motivation for her to care about how her customers feel. She is simply performing her duty and does not have to show deference to customers. In a privately owned store, we find a totally different distribution of power. The customer, who has the money, is the one with power. This is clearly the case in the privately owned women's clothing store, as exemplified by the saleswoman's treatment of her customers. She is highly motivated to create a friendly atmosphere for their interaction to please them.

Larger societal changes produce a shift in power relations in service. This change, in turn, affects the way facework is applied in the interaction between service people and their customers. If we just look at politeness behavior in Chinese service encounters without analyzing the social conditions under which these interactions take place, we can form at most a partial picture. We need to look at politeness behavior from a historic perspective. China's economy is going through a transitional period, and interpersonal relationships also show a mixture of every element: traditional, state-socialist, and free economy. Politeness strategies employed in day-to-day life encode these elements. Study of language in its actual use allows us to see not only how linguistic politeness is used, but also the social forces underlying politeness phenomena in a given society.

4

"WHO IS THE BOSS?" HIERARCHICAL STRUCTURE IN AN OFFICIAL SETTING

To this day, I remember a comment made by the Finnish diplomat whom I mentioned in chapter 1. Finnish business people always asked her the question of how not to lose face or upset the Chinese face in China. She said to them: "You don't have to worry too much about that. You know what, foreigners don't have face in China, because they don't belong to the system." The system she referred to is the face system in Chinese culture. A face system, part of a discourse system, is the way a social group organizes relationships among the members of its group (Scollon & Scollon, 1995). It includes how kinship is viewed, how self is perceived in relation to others, the relationship between ingroup and outgroup members, and the relationship between local community and society. The face system governs the interactive norm among members of the group, and the interactive norm between ingroup and outgroup members. As we explored in the last two chapters, social distance has a decisive weight in politeness behavior in the initial stage of an interpersonal contact in Chinese culture. There is a differential treatment of kin and nonkin, friend and stranger, fellow Chinese and foreigners. The concept of face is relevant only when someone is in the inside system, and facework is then called for to address the face need of an insider in accordance with the perceived hierarchical order between the two interactants. That is why the Finnish diplomat said to her countrymen that foreigners don't have face in China, because foreigners (*waiguoren,* "outside country person") are, in every sense of the word, outsiders. They are not expected to act the same way as Chinese and allowances are made for their social conduct.

The distinction between inside and outside is like a series of concentric circles. The inner most circle is the most intimate relationship consisting of family members and relatives; further circles are friends, fellow villagers, co-workers, colleagues, and acquaintances. Within these circles, the social factor of hierarchy comes into the picture, and face consideration becomes important in the interaction. Although China is a highly hierarchical society with patriarchy and seniority as the basis for the social structure (Zhao & Gao, 1990), the hierarchical structure is relevant for face concern mainly in inside relationships. The five classical Confucian relationships (ruler-ruled, father-son, husband-wife, elder-younger, friend-friend) are all based on the inside circle of relation. They encode the hierarchical order in social relations, with authority, male gender, and age seniority in the superordinate position in the hierarchy.

The term "hierarchy," however, should be understood in its cultural context here. In the Chinese context, "hierarchy" does not hold a win-or-lose connotation. In the Chinese mind, every individual exists in a paired relation to others, like *yin* and *yang* (the moon and the sun). This paired relation calls for a harmonious coexistence and strong unity among individuals. Group harmony and unity became the basic face needs for the Chinese. In order to achieve these, every individual should acknowledge the relative hierarchical order in the pair and follow the Confucian behavior code of *zun zhang ai you* (Be respectful to the old and benevolent to the young). Here "the old" and "the young" indicate more than just age. By association, *zhang* (the old) extends to anyone with seniority and authority in age, rank, or social status. *You* (the young), on the other hand, is associated with lack of seniority. The principle of "be respectful to the old and benevolent to the young" thus includes the interactive norm of hierarchy and the concept of paired relationship between participants and can be considered to be the basic rule for polite behavior and social interaction in Chinese culture. The question is, in a particular situation, what source of power is recognized as the dominant one when several social factors compete with each other. In other words, what does a person need to know in order to be placed in the *zhang* (superordinate) position, and how do people react to power difference following the rules of politeness in the Chinese context? I show in this chapter that hierarchy in the official setting is based upon the rank system and that the power coming from rank overrides the power coming from other factors such as age and gender.

HIERARCHICAL STRUCTURE IN THE OFFICIAL SETTING

The government ranking system in Chinese society has a long tradition, dating back to the Qin Dynasty (221–206 B.C.). Government officials always enjoyed the highest social status and power in ancient China. The four traditional categories of social class are *shi, nong, gong, shang* (officials, farmers, workers, and businessmen) with officials occupying the highest position. With the socialist reform movement following the founding of the People's Republic of China in 1949, a cadre system was adopted in all social sectors, using the government official ranking system from Grade 1 to Grade 26 with Grade 1 as the highest. This system applied not only to employees of government organizations, but also to employees of other institutions such as banks, hospitals, universities, schools, state-run stores, and business companies. The salary system was made uniform across the country based on this ranking system. Up until the economic reform in the 1980s, there were basically two salary systems: the cadre system and the worker system. Those working in factories were on the worker salary system, and those working in the government and various institutions were on the cadre system. So the whole society was invisibly divided into these two big social groups.

Those who were under the cadre system had much more social status and enjoyed more privileges than those on the worker system. In addition to higher salaries than the working class, the cadre class has access to political and material benefits based on the rank, including access to certain types of newspapers, government information, job opportunities, housing, and many other kinds of allowances. To a certain extent an individual's value was based on, and judged by, the rank he/she occupied. These privileges combined with the traditional prestige attached to government officials made rank one of the most important yardsticks measuring an individual's status and power in socialist China, especially before the 1979 economic opening and reform movement. It is true that this attitude has changed somewhat since the economic reform in 1979, as money becomes more and more important and official rank loses some of its past significance. However, the power and privilege that come with official rank still cannot be replaced by other things.

Thus, the ranking hierarchy is the foremost factor to consider in politeness behavior in an official setting. The term "official setting" is used to include government organizations and companies and professions operated by the government. In this chapter I look at business meetings conducted in the official setting to illustrate how official rank emerges as a prominent influence on politeness phenomena in the workplace. Business meetings as a form of discourse provide perspective on the study of language and society because of the role relationship, power relations and cultural values evident in the process of a meeting. Gu and Zhu (1996) outlined three kinds of power (political, administrative, and expert) in China by examining business meetings. Yamada (1992, 1997) compared the cultural values of American and Japanese society based on bank business meetings.

In terms of politeness behavior, business meetings are a good place to observe how participants with different ranks interact, what norms are being observed, what procedure is being followed and finally, what face strategies are employed to signal the differences in power among the participants. In previous studies (Pan, 1995, 1996a, 1996b), I found that politeness behavior in an official setting is indicated by participants' acknowledgment of rank difference and power relations. Participants position themselves in relation to others in accordance with their ranking positions in the hierarchy. Participants' roles are clearly defined and speech activities follow the hierarchical order. This behavior shares a similar pattern with Japanese culture in which relation acknowledgment is a fundamental force underlying politeness behavior. Under this cultural norm, "it is crucial for a speaker to perceive the social context, such as the kind of situation or setting s/he is in, what kind of social relation s/he has with other participants in the communication, the social status, and position in the conversation, etc., and to show recognition of that social context" (Matsumoto, 1988, pp. 421-422). It is by acknowledging the addressee's rank position (either higher or lower than the speaker) in the official setting that speakers show their politeness. This connection between position acknowledgment and politeness strategies is indicated in the conversational features of topic opening/closing flow, decision making, management of conflict talk, and the use of address forms. I shall elaborate these points in the following sections.

MEETING/TOPIC OPENING
FLOW AND SPEAKING PATTERN

Most business meetings in my data follow a similar pattern in opening a meeting or a topic. That is, the person highest in ranking position (#1 person) opens the meeting/topic with an introductory remark. Then #1 passes the topic to #2 (the one that comes second in rank). #2 gives details about the topic and opens the discussion. Discussion then follows among other participants, mostly without #1, who remains silent during most of the discussion. #1 does not take up many speaking turns and is not the most voluble speaker in a meeting, but he/she speaks at critical moments to make a decision or to end an argument.

The following excerpt is from a municipal youth committee meeting. Lao is the secretary of the committee and is #1 in the rank hierarchy at the meeting. He announces the opening of the meeting and gives a brief introduction to the agenda, then passes the floor to Fan, the deputy secretary of the committee, who is #2 at the meeting.

Example 4.1.   Lao is concluding his introduction of the agenda for the meeting

    1. Lao: *Gam2 daai6 tai2 soeng6 gam1 jat6 haa6 ng5*
                      so general up today afternoon

2.   *zau6 gam2 joeng6 ge2 on1 paai4.*
           Just this-way GW agenda

3.   *Aa1 gam2 sin1 gaau2 dai6 jat1 daan1 je5*
           TW so first do first MW thing

4.   *zau6 hai2 jung6 nei1 go3...*
           just be use this

5.   *nei5 nei1 dou3 gong2 aa1, hai2 m4 hai2?*
           you here speak TW be not be

           So, this is basically the agenda for this afternoon.
           And, we're going to deal with the first issue,
           that is, to use …
           Here, you'll speak first. Is that right?

6. Fan: *Hai2, ngo5 nei1 dou3 gong2 gong2 sin1naa4*
           yes I here speak speak first TW

7.   *hou2 m4 hou2 ?*
           Okay not Okay

           Right, I'll speak first, Okay?

8. Lao: *Gam2, zau6 Fan3 syu1 gei3 naa3, sin1 gong2 gong2*
           so then Fan secretary TW first speak speak

9.   *go3 jaa6 gau2 hou6 zou2 san4 ge2 on1 paai4 sin1*
           that 29 number morning GW plan first

           Well, then, Secretary Fan is going to talk about the schedule for
           the morning of the 29th.

           (Fan continues to talk about the schedule. Other participants
           join him for discussion)

When the meeting starts, Lao makes some brief introductory remarks about the meeting agenda, and opens the topic for discussion by saying "we're going to deal with the first issue" (line 2, 3). He then asks Fan to lead the discussion. Fan, the one who gets the floor, does not even try to do so on his own initiative. The floor is simply passed to him from his superior. He restates that he will speak first and seeks acknowledgment from his superior. He uses the phrase "*hou m hou?*" (literal meaning "okay not okay?") with a question intonation, which is mainly used to ask for permission. Lao confirms his request and formally passes the floor to Fan (lines 8-9). The discussion goes on among the participants while Lao stays out of it most of the time.

During the meeting, the #1 person maintains a low profile. He plays the role of mediator, trying to make sure that the meeting is going on smoothly. The participant

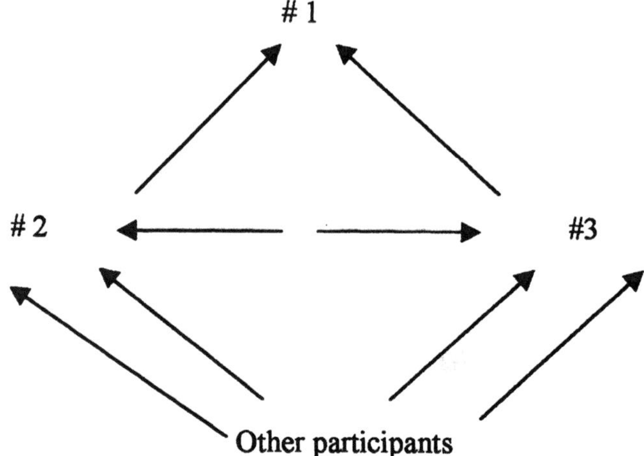

FIGURE 4.1.   Speaking Pattern

TABLE 4.1.   Turns Taken by Six Participants at an Internal Bank Business Meeting

Participants	Number of turns	*Percentage*
Bank manager (male)	32	14%
Department director (male)	65	29%
Deputy director (female)	54	24%
Other three participants	54	24%
Total	224	100%

who speaks the most is not the #1 person, but the #2 and the #3. The #2 person functions as the spokesman for the #1 person, and #3 raises questions and brings up different opinions. Most of the discussions and arguments occur between these two people, with other participants lower in rank occasionally giving supporting ideas and details to one of the two opposing sides. #2 and #3, as well as other participants, defer to the #1 person as soon as he says something. Figure 4.1 illustrates this pattern.

This pattern indicates the order of speaking during a meeting, which is associated with the speaker's rank. Let us look at the turn-taking pattern in a bank business meeting to see who takes up most speaking turns during the meeting. There are six people at this meeting discussing the selection of model employees in the company. We notice that #2 and #3 are most active in volunteering speaking turns, and #1 only takes up a small percentage of speaking turns. The other three participants do not contribute much to the meeting. Table 4.1 shows the number of turns taken by the six participants at the meeting.

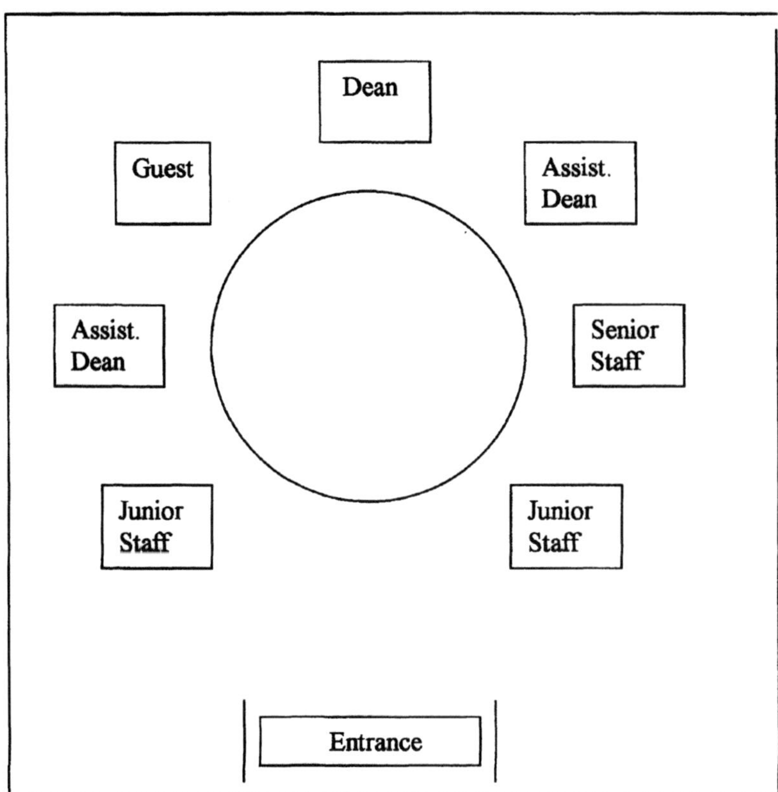

FIGURE 4.2.   Seating Arrangement of an Official Dinner

As the table indicates, most of the discussion takes place between the director and the deputy director. The bank manager does not speak as much as the two directors. The other three participants (two men and one woman) together take up a total of 24 percent of all the speaking turns. They are not as active during the meeting and just make comments on the points raised by #2 or #3. One point worth mentioning is that there is no great difference in the number of turns taken by male and female participants. If a female speaker is in a high enough position, she is entitled to certain speaking rights. As shown in Table 4.1, the female deputy director talks much more than the other three participants (two men and one woman), and nearly as much as the male director. This indicates that the factor of gender does not affect speaking rights as much as rank does. The topic opening flow follows a pattern correlated with rank hierarchy, and each speaker's speaking right is tied to his/her position. To act with appropriate social etiquette in this situation is to recognize this subtle pattern and follow the rules of when to speak and how much to talk. If a subordinate speaks at the wrong moment, it is considered improper and impolite.

This pattern applies not only to official meetings in the workplace but also to other official social events. At one official dinner given in my honor when I gave a lecture at a Chinese university, the dinner-table conversation showed a speaking pattern similar to that described above. The participants took turns speaking in accordance with their rank, especially at the beginning of the dinner. During the dinner, however, one junior staff member asked me a question about doing research and then made a relatively lengthy comment on how difficult it was to write a research paper. The dean later apologized to me, saying that the junior staff member didn't know how to be polite (*bu dong limao*), because during this occasion it was not his turn to speak (*lun bu dao ta shuohua*). The junior staff member clearly spoke so much that it violated the norm of social etiquette on this occasion. This shows how important it is to observe the speaking pattern in an official situation.

The seating arrangement (see Figure 4.2) also reflected the hierarchy-oriented pattern at the dinner. The dean (#1 in the rank hierarchy among the participants) sat at the center of a big round table, facing the entrance of a separate dining room in a big restaurant. The guest of honor was on his right hand side. The first assistant dean (#2 in the hierarchy) sat on his left hand side, then another assistant dean, #3 in the hierarchy, to the right of the guest of honor, one senior staff member, #4, to the left of the first assistant dean (#2), and then the two junior staff members near the entrance. Like the speaking pattern, the seating arrangement is tied to rank.

What does all of this tell us about politeness behavior in a meeting? The topic opening flow reflects the power distribution among the speakers. Speaking rights among speakers are pre-determined by their position in the rank hierarchy. Speakers talk according to this pre-determined allocation of speaking rights. Who speaks first, and who speaks next, and how much they can speak are decided by their position. To be polite and act appropriately in this situation means to follow the speaking rules and the order and not to step over the line. Speakers should know where they stand in relation to others and speak according to their position. If a speaker occupies the most important position in a meeting, he/she controls the floor, but does not get very involved in the discussion. If a speaker comes second or third in the ranking position, he/she is entitled to contribute most to the discussion. Other participants participate in the discussion whenever they see it is appropriate for them to make a contribution.

TOPIC CLOSING

Just as the topic opening flow shows the connection between power hierarchy and speaking rights, the topic closing also follows a pattern that indicates power dif-

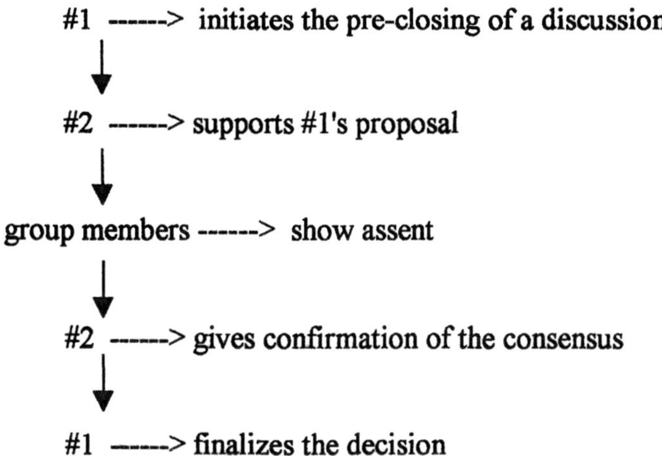

FIGURE 4.3.   Steps in Topic-Closing Process

ferentiation among the speakers. During the discussion session of a meeting, the #1 person stays out of most of the discussion and participants can give different opinions. When it comes to the point of closing the discussion of a topic, however, the speaker's position in the rank hierarchy determines his/her choice of face-maintenance strategies in concluding the topic. The most powerful person in the group is always the one that initiates and finalizes decisions, using bald on-record face strategies. Those of lower rank give "face" to him by supporting his position, using deferential face strategies.

The steps taken in closing a topic can be briefly described as follows. The person with the highest rank (#1) makes the initial step by drawing some kind of conclusion from the discussion, and his opinion is echoed by other group members. Usually the person that comes second in the rank hierarchy (#2) will show his/her support. Then other group members show agreement. After that, #2 summarizes and confirms the group's consensus, and then #1 finalizes the decision. Figure 4.3 is a visual presentation of the steps taken in making a decision. Since we are focusing here on the topic-closing process, the discussion session is omitted from the figure.

Although it is not surprising that the most powerful person initiates and finalizes decisions, what is interesting here is that the power hierarchy among the participants is indicated by the steps each participant takes in the decision-making process. Each time #1 makes the initial attempt for a decision, #2 immediately either rephrases or repeats what is said by #1. Then other members lower in rank speak in chorus to give their agreement, usually by a single lexical item indicating agreement (for example, OK), which shows their acknowledgment of the power and status of their superior, even if they may not agree or totally agree with the decision. This reflects how deference is given in a hierarchical scale.

The following excerpt is a typical example of such a decision-making process taken from a municipal committee meeting concerning the youth league committee work. When discussing the best way to publicize the plans of the youth league committee, participants give different opinions during the discussion session. After some discussion, the deputy secretary, Fan (#2 in the group), mentions that they could publicize the plan by publishing a special issue of the youth league newspaper. Lao (#1) finalizes the plan and closes the topic:

Example 4.2.   making a decision

   1. Fan: *Keoi5 nei1 ci3 m4 hai6 zung6 jiu3 gaau2*
              they this time not be also need make

   2.   *go3 dak6 hon1 maa3 ?*
              MW special issue QW

              Aren't they (the youth league committee newspaper) going to have a special issue this time?

   3. Lao: *Aa2 ?*
              TW

              What?

   4. Fan: *Nei5 zung6 jiu3 gaau2 go3 dak6 hon1 ...*
              you still need make MW special issue

              You still need to have a special issue ...

   5. Lao: *Gon1 ceoi3 gaau2 go3 dak6 hon1*
              simply make MW special issue

              Yes, (we) can simply publish a special issue.

   6. Fan: *Gaau2 go3 dak6 hon1 m4 zau6 dak1 laa1*
              make MW special issue not just Okay TW

              A special issue will do.

   7. Lao: *Hou2 m4 hou2 ?*
              good not good

              Is that okay?

   8. Rong: *Zeoi3 hou2 laa1, gam2 joeng6*
              most good TW this way

              That's the best way.

9. Lili: *Hou2 wa1*
              good TW

              That's good

10. Fan: *Gaau2 go3 dak6 hon1.*
              make MW special issue

              Publish a special issue.

11. Lao: *Nei5 go1 dou3 ne1 zau6 sin3 gaau2 dim6 sin3*
              you there TW then first make complete first

              You take care of everything there first.

12. Fan: *Aa3*
              TW

              Yes.

13. Lao: *Aa3, gam2 nei2 dou3ne1, go3 bou6 sat1*
              TW so here TW every department office

14.   *zoi3 gaau2 go3 dak6 hon1*
              again make MW special issue

              And, then, here, every department and office has to contribute to the
              special issue.

When Fan (#2) brings up the idea of a special issue to publicize the work plan,
Lao seems to like the suggestion. Line 5 shows Lao's intention to conclude the
discussion on this issue. He states it in an affirmative sentence ("Yes, (we) can
simply publish a special issue," line 5), giving the impression of authority in the
matter, thus generating the initiation for conclusion. Fan gives his support for
Lao's position in line 6 ("A special issue will do"). Then Lao asks other members'
opinion to get consensus. Because of the group-oriented nature of Chinese society
(Liu & Lin, 1988), Chinese speakers tend to be concerned with achieving some
kind of consensus, which leads to harmony within the group. Thus, once #1
expresses his opinion as the concluding remark, all other members show deference
and agree with him. Then #2, Fan, confirms the consensus ("Publish a special
issue," line 10), and #1 finalizes the decision and gives orders to his subordinates
to carry out the action (line 11 and lines 13–14).

The following example also shows how when the top person talks other participants applaud his idea. After a period of discussion, the top person is ready to close
the topic, and his decision is elaborated and completed by other group members in
the manner of indirectly speaking for him. I use the term "continued dialogue" to
refer to the phenomenon that the current speaker is adding more information to the
other's utterance, either by repetition, interpretation, or elaboration. On the surface

level, continued dialogue seems to be the discourse by the current speaker. A closer look at it will reveal that the continued dialogue is the discourse of another enacted by the current speaker in that the speaker is interpreting the other's discourse in the way preferred by the other. The speaker is speaking for the superior. When the superior makes an initial attempt to close the topic, other group members show their support by completing his sentences. Example 4.3 illustrates that a superior's utterance is repeated, elaborated and completed by other speakers in the group.

Example 4.3.   At a city committee meeting, discussing the deadline for a project
Participants: Lao—(male) secretary, 35
Fan—(male) deputy secretary, 28
Lou—(male) staff member, 30
Wong—(male) staff member, 25

1. Lao: *Ngo5 deng6 go3 jat6 zi2.*
I set MW date

I'll set a deadline.

2. Wong: *Deng2 go3 jat6 zi2 laa1.*
set MW date TW

Yes, set a deadline.

3. Lou: *Deng2 go3 jat6zi2, lo2dou3 co1bou6 ji3gin3.*
set MW date get initial idea

4.   *faan1 heoi3 cyu2lei5, hou2 m4 hou2?*
go back handle good not good

Set a deadline. Get some initial ideas and go back to work, OK?

5. Wong: *M4 hai6, jau5 go3 si4 gaan3 hou2 zou6 si6.*
not be have MW time good do thing

6.   *Mou5 go3 si4gaan3, m4 zi1 gei2si4.*
not-have MW time not know when

No, have a set time so that we can do things.
If (we) don't have a deadline, (we) don't know when (to do things)

7. Fan: *Ngo5 tai2 gam2 joeng6 hou2 m4 hou2,*
I see such good not good

8.   *tau4sin1 Lao6 syu1 gei3 gong2 zo2 hou2 do1.*
just-now Lao secretary say GW very much

9.   *Zau6 hai6 jat 6 zi2 jiu3 ming4 nin4,*
that be date need next-year

10.   *ji4 ce2 jiu3 hai2 ngo5 dei6, ni1go3 ...*
             moreover need at our this ...

             Let me say this, OK? Just now Secretary Lao has talked a lot.
             That is, the deadline has to be next year and has to be at our ...
             this ...

11. Lao: *Cyun4-wai1 wui5 cin4.*
             committee meeting before

             Before the committee meeting.

12. Fan: *Cyun4-wai1 wui5. Cyun4-wai1 wui5 cin4.*
             committee meeting committee meeting before

13.   *Cyun4-wai1 wui5 cin4. Gam2, wai4 zo2 bin6 jyu1 ngo5 dei6*
             committee meeting before. So in-order-to facilitate we

14.   *zou6 ding6 gei3waak6, ji4 ce2 wai4 zo2 bin6jyu1 ngo5 dei6*
             make decide plan moreover in-order-to facilitate we

15.   *zou6 ding6 bei6 gaau1 lok6 sat6 ge3 gei3waak6,*
             make decide relatively firm GW plan

16.   *ngo5 ge3 ji3 si1 ne1 zau6 hai6 m4 hai6 hai2 baat3 hou4 cin4,*
             my idea TW just be not be on eight number before

17.   *baat3 hou4 cin4 go3 bou6mun4*
             eight number before each department

18.   *zing2 ne1 go3 gung1 zok3 gei3 waak6 ding6 ceot1 lei4.*
             make this work plan decide out

             Committee meeting, before the committee meeting, before the
             committee meeting... So in order to facilitate making a plan,
             moreover, in order to facilitate making a relatively firm plan,
             my idea is that if it is OK that before the 8th, before the 8th,
             each department works out this work plan.

In this meeting, Lao occupies the highest rank position among all the participants. But in this extract, he said just two sentences: line 1, "I'll set a deadline,"
and line 11, "Before the committee meeting." His ideas are acted out by other participants at the meeting. The two staff members, Wong and Lou, repeat Lao's
utterance ("Set a deadline"), and then go on to give their interpretation of why a
specific date should be set (lines 3-4 and lines 5-6). Lou says that by having a
deadline, they will know what to work on, while Wong says that by having a deadline, they will know when to do their work. Both are providing supportive details
to Lao's utterance. They are speaking for the superior to elaborate on and interpret

his wishes. Then Fan, the person that comes second in the rank hierarchy, continues what Lao has left out. Fan starts by saying "Let me say this, OK" and then speaks for Lao about setting a date for working out the plan. When Lao says "Before the committee meeting" (line 9), Fan repeats it three times, which indicates he is acting on Lao's behalf. Then Fan talks about the importance of setting a deadline and suggests a date for the completion of the task. Here, he is presenting input that is the preferred decision of a superior. Lao, the superior, does not have to say anything more, because other speakers have provided enough information to elaborate his idea.

The strategy of speaking for the other serves two purposes in terms of face concern. First, when speaking for the other, the speaker (in a lower position) is the representation of the other (in a higher position) and the hierarchy. The importance of higher authority is emphasized through the voice of the current speaker, who animates and constructs the other's speech in a way that shows deference to the other (the superior). Thus speaking for the other in a higher position functions to enhance the face of the person being spoken for by acknowledging his/her superiority and avoiding putting oneself first. Second, speaking for the other can frame the speaker in a position of neutrality; he/she is producing the speech for others instead of directly stating his/her own ideas. The current speaker is downplaying his/her own importance as well as responsibility. This indirectness in discourse could reduce direct confrontation among group members, especially in a meeting where consensus is seen as the goal. Participants at a meeting use this strategy to produce utterances which they think might have some impact on the audience, particularly when saying something that is likely to cause potential tension.

The correlation of rank hierarchy and linguistic behavior in the decision-making process is another example of how institutionalized power affects language use in Chinese official settings. This behavioral pattern can be traced to the historical pattern of autocratic government in traditional Chinese society as well as the practice of "democratic centralism" under the Communist government beginning in the 1940s in Yanan. In China's history, the emperor was the #1 person in the government and his word was the law. Though the emperor did hold discussions on national affairs with his officials, he was always the one that finalized decisions. The tradition obviously still lingers on and affects linguistic behavior in today's Chinese society. The Communist government adopted the system of "democratic centralism" as the legislative procedure to regulate opinions and formulate the party's policy. Under this system, lower level members can give their opinions during a discussion and it is the duty of the superior to listen to those opinions. The superior then summarizes different opinions and exercises the power to make decisions. The system was designed to serve a two-fold ideal aim of achieving democracy while maintaining the authority of those in power. The topic opening and closing flow in an official meeting seem to embody this democratic centralism.

MANAGEMENT OF CONFLICT TALK

Conflict talk is a distinctive speech activity. "In verbal conflict, participants oppose the utterances, actions, or selves of one another in successive turns at talk" (Vuchinich, 1990, p. 118). How conflict talk is managed in a given context is closely associated with social variables such as the power/status hierarchy and social distance (Grimshaw, 1990). It is found in the present study that directness in expressing opposition is correlated with power distribution in Chinese official meetings. That is, the person with the highest rank is most direct in stating his opposition. A person lower in rank tends to stay away from direct confrontation by using linguistic strategies that mitigate the imposition of an opposing turn. Mitigation, as Ng and Bradac (1993) point out, "is to signal to the addressee that the speaker's intention behind an unwelcome communication has been softened" (p. 92). The subordinate's tendency to mitigate an opposing turn indicates his/her deference toward the addressee in a higher power position.

The following excerpt is a discussion about what to buy as an award for prize winners in a current events contest sponsored by a municipal youth league committee. Five people participate in this discussion: Lao, Fan, Tai, Lili and Rong. Lao occupies the highest position in terms of rank hierarchy. Fan comes second. Tai, Lili and Rong are equals, and Lili is the only female speaker. During the discussion session, conflict occurs when Fan, the deputy secretary, brings up a suggestion of getting photo albums. Participants give their opinions, and different suggestions are offered and debated. Lao, the secretary, often states his opposition in a direct, terse way without giving any reason or argument; he simply vetoes the suggestion made by the previous speaker. Other participants do not state their opposition directly. Instead, they give reasons for not favoring a particular suggestion, or bring up an alternative as a way to show their opposition. The conflict terminates with Fan's reintroduction of his suggestion. Other participants show no objection, and the suggestion is finalized by Lao. This illustrates how linguistic choices for stating opinions and opposition are related to the rank hierarchy among the participants. Since it is important to have some idea of the whole process in which a decision is reached after quite a few opposition turn exchanges, I will give this long example first and then present my analysis. References to specific lines will be made in the course of my analysis.

Example 4.4.   Discussing what to buy as an award for prize winners in the current events contest

Participants (presented in order of rank):
            Lao (male), secretary, age 34
            Fan (male), deputy secretary, age 28
            Tai (male), department head, age 30

Lili (female), department head, age 28
Rong (male), department head, age 30

1. Fan: *Maai5 soeng2 bou6.*
buy photo album

Let's buy photo albums

2. Tai: *Maai5 cat1 man1 ge2 go3 di1 dou1 ho2 ji5, jiu3 gwo2 hai2…*
buy seven dollar more those also can if be

(We) can also buy seven- or eight-dollar ones, if it's …

3. Lao: *M4 jat1 ding6 go3 di1. Dou1 hou2 gwo3 nei5 maai5.*
not necessary those all good than you buy

4.   *sei3 ng5 man1 go3 di1, faan2 zeng3 dou1 hai2 jau6 peng4.*
four five dollar those anyway also be still cheap

Not necessarily those. But they're better than four- or five-dollar
ones. Anyway, seven dollars is still cheap.

5. Tai: *Maai5 ho6 nin4 kaat1 laa1.*
buy new-year card TW

Well, buy some New Year's cards.

6. Lao: *M4 hou2.*
no good

That's no good.

7. Lili: *Sei2 laa1, jat1 man1 gai1 jat1 go3. Zan1 hai2 gam2 juk6syun1,*
dead TW one dollar one MW really be so ugly

8.   *go3 di1 ho6 nin4 kaat1, jat1 man1…*
those new-year card one dollar

My god! That's only one dollar each. Those New Year's cards
are really ugly, one dollar …

9. Tai: *M4 hai6, jau5 di1 ho6 nin4 kaat1 sap6 gei2 man1*
not be some new-year card ten more dollar

10.   *jat1 go3 dou1 jau5.*
one MW also have

No, some New Year's cards are over ten dollars each.

11. Lili: *Jat1 man1 gei2.*
one dollar more

Just over one dollar.

12. Lao: *M4 hou2.*
no good

That's no good.

13. Tai: *Maai5 go3 di1 maau1 zai2, luk6 man1 jat1 deoi3.*
buy those kitty six dollar one pair

Buy some kitties then. Six dollars per pair.

14. Fan: *Maau1 zai2 jau5 mat1 je5 jung6 ?*
kitty have what use

What's the use of kitties?

15. Tai: *Tou4 ci4 maau1 zai2 maa5!*
6 ceramic kitty TW

Ceramic kitties!

16. Fan: *Hai6, jau5 mat1 je5 jung6 ?*
TW have what use

Yeah, but what's the use?

17. Tai: *Lei4 tai2 maa5. Ngaam1 m4 ngaam1 ?*
to look TW appropriate not appropriate

Just to look at. Isn't it appropriate?

18. Fan: *Jiu4 gwo2 jiu3 heoi2 maai5, maai5 toi4 lik6 faan1 lei4.*
if need go buy buy desk calendar back

If (we) have to buy something, buy some desk calendars then.

19. Lili: *Maai5 mat1 je5 ?*
buy what

Buy what?

20. Fan: *Maai5 toi4 lik6 faan1 lei4.*
buy desk calendar back

Buy desk calendars.

21. Lili: *Toi4 lik6 hou2 do1 jan4 jau5 laa1. Hou2 do1 jan4,*
desk calendar very many people have TW very many people

22.   *zik1 hai6 wu6 soeng1 do1 jau5 jan4 sung3.*
that-is mutually all have people send

23.   *Gam2 nei5 lo2 gam3 do1 zou6 mat1 je5 waa1 ?*
then you get so many do what TW

24.   *gwaa3 lik6, toi 4 lik6 do1 gwo3 tau4*
hanging calendar desk calendar much too much

Lots of people already have desk calendars, y'know.
Many people send desk calendars to each other (as gifts).
Then, what's the use of having so many (calendars)?
People have too many wall calendars and desk calendars.

25. Rong: *Ngo5, ngo5 cyun4 zo2 hou2 do1, hou2 do1 go3 dik1toi4 lik6.*
I I save GW very many very many those desk calendar

Yeah, I, I've collected many, many calendars.

26. Lili: *Gwaa3 lik6, toi lik6 hou2 do1.*
hanging calendar desk calendar very many

(People have) many wall calendars and desk calendars.

27. Lao: *Mou5 so2 wai4 ge2, maai5 toi4 lik6.*
No matter TW buy desk calendar

It's still okay to buy desk calendars.

28. Lili: *Nei5 ji4 gaa1 zi3 hai6, ji4 gaa1 nei1 go3 si4 hau6*
you now that be now this time

29.   *hou2 do1 jan4 sung3*
very many people send

But, at this time (of the year) many people send each other calendars.

30. Tai: *Maai5 dik1 gung1 ngai6 ban2 jik6 dak1 ze1*
buy some handicraft item also Okay TW

31.   *gung1 ngai6 ban2 laa1*
handicraft item TW

It will also do to buy some handicraft items.
Yes, handicraft items.

32. Lili: *Gung1 ngai6 ban2, nei1 go3 dik1 ling5 dou6*
handicraft item you those leader

33.   *gung1 ngai6 ban2, gam1...sat6 hai6*
handicraft item so really

Handicraft items to give those leaders!
How could we give them handicraft items? Really so …

34. Lao: *M4 hai6, keoi5 go3 dik1 ...dak6 jiu1 gun1zung3*
no be they those specially invited audience

35.   *lei6 dou3 zo6 zyu6 jat1 leon4...*
                 come arrive sit GW one round

                 That's not good. Those honorable guests come and sit there for
                 sometime ...

36. Fan: *Waak6 ze2 jat1 jyu1 hai6 soeng2 bou6 laa1. Heoi3, heoi3*
                  or just be photo album TW go go

                  Or just get photo albums. Why not? Go, go ...

37. Rong: *Soeng2 bou6 ge2 hou2. Jau5 mat1 je5 m4 hou2*
                  photo album so good have what no good

                  Photo albums are good. Why not get photo albums?

38. Lili: *Hou2 waa1, mou5 waa6 m4 hou2 waa3*
                  good TW not say no good TW

                  Okay. I didn't say it's no good.

39. Lao: *Hai6 hou2, sai3 sai3 ge2. Sap6 ng5 man1 go1 zung2*
                  be good small small GW fifteen dollar that kind

                  Yes, it's good. Those small cute ones, those kind that are
                  fifteen dollars each.

40. Fan: *Hai1, zoi3 heoi3 lo2 do1 gei2 bun2*
                  yes again go get more few volume

41.   *soeng2 bou6 faan1 lei6 hai6 laa1*
                  photo album back be TW

                  Right. Let's just go and get a few more photo albums.

A linguistic analysis shows that there are four ways of stating opposition in this
conflict talk used by the participants:

1. Giving direct opposition using the negative expressions of *m hai* (not be) or
    m hou (no good) to deny the previous suggestion.
2. Challenging a previous suggestion by showing doubt and downplaying the
    proposition. For example, Fan opposes Tai's suggestion in line 16: "What's
    the use of kitties?"
3. Reasoning without directly stating one's position. This is a strategy to avoid
    direct confrontation. The speaker just makes a statement about the object
    being discussed, or states some facts without saying whether he/she agrees or
    disagrees with the suggestion. The speaker's opinion is actually implied in
    the words being used, as shown by their connotation (whether derogatory or
    recommendatory). For instance, when Tai mentions buying New Year's

cards, Lili (lines 9–10) emphasizes how cheap and ugly those New Year's cards are, implying that such a cheap and ugly item is not appropriate to be given as an award.

4. Providing alternatives. That is, instead of overtly disagreeing with a previous speaker, the current speaker provides a new suggestion as an alternative. It draws the attention of the listeners to a new idea. As a result, the dispute over the previous one is neglected.

These four strategies are in descending order in terms of directness of opposition. The use of these strategies is clearly associated with power distribution. Lao, the person highest in rank, uses direct opposition most often. Three out of four of his opposition turns (lines 8, 14, 38–39) are direct opposition (for example, "That's no good," line 8). Furthermore, he does not provide any reason for his opposition—he is simply exercising his power as the one that gives approval or disapproval.

Fan, occupying the second highest position in the rank hierarchy, also comes second in terms of directness in expressing opposition. In his three opposition turns (lines 16, 18 and 20–21), he challenges Tai's suggestion of buying ceramic kitties in two of his utterances ("What's the use of kitties?" lines 16 and 18). In lines 20–21, Fan gives a conditional alternative ("If we have to buy something, buy some desk calendars then"). But it is not easy for him to give up his position. In line 40, he brings up his idea of getting photo albums again. And this time, consensus is achieved.

The only female speaker in the conflict is Lili. She is not, however, the most indirect person in airing opposition. Nor does she withdraw from conflict as females do in other domains (for example, the family setting). Her strategy is to give reasons without openly stating direct opposition. Such a strategy serves two purposes: to state opposition and to avoid direct confrontation. For example, when objecting to Fan's suggestion of buying desk calendars, instead of saying it is a bad idea, she states that people already have too many of them since people send each other calendars as New Year's gifts.[9] Then she poses the question of "What's the use of having so many calendars?" (lines 24–27). Her argument pattern falls into what Young (1982) describes as the Chinese argumentation norm of building up one's reasons before giving one's opinion.

Tai uses the strategy of giving alternatives in most of his opposition turns (lines 7, 15, 34–35). He does not defend his position when his suggestion is challenged. Instead, he keeps bringing up alternatives from New Year's cards (line 7) to ceramic kitties (line 15) to handicraft articles (line 34–35). Giving alternatives also indicates a tendency to stay away from the confrontation, an act deemed appropriate for a subordinate in the Chinese context. The speaker does not want to pursue the argument of right or wrong, good or bad. Tai actually does withdraw when Fan reintroduces his suggestion in line 40 and everybody else expresses assent. Tai is the one that does not say anything at that point, which indicates his tacit acceptance of Fan's suggestion.

Rong is the least active in the conflict, though his status is equal to that of Tai or Lili. He just provides a supporting statement (lines 28–29) to Lili's argument that people already have too many calendars and agrees with Fan's suggestion of buying photo albums toward the end of the conflict (line 41). He remains silent during the most part of the discussion, and silence is most likely to be interpreted as assent rather than dissent for someone in a lower position in Chinese culture.

Other conflict talk found in my data shows a similar pattern to that described in the above example. That is, the higher a speaker's rank, the more direct he is in expressing opposition. Participants of a lower rank have to modify their opposition to some degree. This is because the power associated with a speaker's rank puts him in a position to "impose" on his addressee, while the subordinates have to be deferential to their superiors and avoid sounding rude. So Lakoff's politeness rule of "don't impose" (Lakoff, 1973) is only a "one-way street" in a Chinese formal situation.

The two other factors of gender and age, on the other hand, do not significantly affect people's politeness behavior in this setting in my data. Lili, the female speaker who participates in the conflict cited in the above example, is not verbally intimidated by men and is certainly not the least direct speaker. This is in accordance with what Hsu (1981) describes as the situation-centered behavior of Chinese, which means that situation tends to overshadow sex differences. In business or formal situations, a Chinese woman who has achieved occupational or professional status "tends to be judged in male eyes by her ability and not by her sex" (Hsu, 1981, p. 62). A woman's institutional role gives her power in a given situation. This again reflects the rank-sensitive nature of official settings. However, in all my official meeting data, there is no example of a woman in the highest position to show how Chinese women talk at that level. It would be interesting to investigate and compare how women and men speak at that level.

SPEAKING UP VERSUS SPEAKING DOWN

The use of politeness strategies sends a certain signal about the relationship between the interlocutors. For instance, independence face strategies emphasize the difference and distance between the interlocutors and at the same time show respect to the addressee. Involvement face strategies, on the other hand, create rapport and closeness between the two people (Tannen, 1986, 1990). Generally speaking, the use of face strategies in face-to-face interaction is reciprocal; both interlocutors use independence strategies when they see themselves as distant, and use involvement strategies when they are close. However, in a situation where social differences and hierarchical structure are emphasized, the use of face strategies is not reciprocal. Scollon and Scollon (1995) call this a hierarchical politeness system. In this system, one speaker (the one with less power) speaks "up" by using independence strategies to show respect and deference to the addressee who has more power. The other speaker (the one with more power) speaks "down" by using involvement strategies to show benevolence and rapport with the person with less power. Therefore, speaking up shows the speaker's attention to the power difference and speaking down means the speaker is assured of his/her power privilege and willing to make the other person feel good by showing rapport. The power difference is acknowledged and emphasized in this politeness system.

The choice of address forms in interpersonal communication is often the first indication of how participants view their relationship. The fact that there is a constant awareness of who is up and who is down in the rank hierarchy in the Chinese official setting is reflected in the nonreciprocal use of address forms among participants. The person higher in rank can address the one lower in rank by a less formal term, for example, an informal address form, such as *Xiao Zhang* (Little Zhang) in Mandarin, or a tone word plus first name or last name in Cantonese, *Ah Wong Zai*. Here *Ah* is the tone word indicating informality. *Wong* is the last name, and *zai* means "little." Quite often, informal terms of address send a message that the participants are close to each other and the social distance between them is small. But this may not be the case in the Chinese official setting, because the use of informal address terms is from the superior to the subordinate, and not the other way around. When a subordinate speaks to a superior, he almost always uses a very formal address term. That is, last name plus title, for example, Secretary Lao, Section Chief Wang, or just the title, Department Head.

Of course, it is not absolute that the superior only uses involvement strategies. My data show that the superior sometimes does use the more formal term of address: full name to talk to the subordinate. The point here is that the superior has the option to speak "down" to show involvement or to use a more formal term to show distance. The superior has it both ways. But the subordinate does not have this option and he/she must show recognition of the superior's status. He/she cannot use the informal term to address a superior to show rapport or closeness even if there is no great social distance between them. When two people communicate in the workplace, they act according to their presumed relationship and position in the rank hierarchy.

Another case of speaking up versus speaking down can be found in the use of polite hedges in directives issued by speakers with rank differences. When a superior issues a directive to a subordinate, he/she tends to employ the bald on-record strategy—the most direct way of speaking without any polite hedges or modality markers. When talking to a superior or to equals, the speaker tends to use polite hedges in directives. The following four examples show the differences between superior-to-subordinate, subordinate-to-superior, and equal-to-equal talk.

In the following example, Yin, a deputy secretary of the municipal committee, is issuing a command to one of his subordinates.

Example 4.5.   Yin (age 28) is talking to a subordinate, Gou (age 33)

    1. Yin: *Wai3, aa3 Gou1 zi3 keong4, daa2 din2 waa2 bei2*
                hey TW Gou Zikeong make call to

    2.   *Cung1 zai2 man6 keoi5 gam1 jat6 lo2 faan1 ce1 mei6*
                Cungzai ask him today get back car not

                Hey, ah, Gou Zi-keong, call Cungzai and ask him if he's got the car back today.

    3. Gou: *Aa3, aa3.*
                TW TW

                Eh, eh.

In this example, Yin is issuing a directive to Gou, one of his subordinates. Though younger then Gou, Yin occupies a higher position. This institutional factor of rank hierarchy gives Yin power to deliver an order without using any polite hedges to reduce the imposition of the directive. Yin just uses a tone word, *wai* (hey), to get the addressee's attention and then directly issues the order.

Furthermore, although Yin calls Gou by his full name *Gou Zi-Keong* instead of using a formal address form like Mr. Gou, or the more respectful form of last name plus title, Section Chief Gou, this does not cause offensive feelings to the addressee. This is because their relationship is acknowledged as superior to subordinate and, most often, no linguistic devices are needed to modify what Brown and Levinson would call face threatening acts from a superior to a subordinate.

Like the choice of address terms, the use of other face strategies depends upon who is up and who is down in the rank hierarchy. The person higher in rank can display authority or claim solidarity by using bald on-record strategies or positive politeness when interacting with a subordinate. Both strategies enhance the superior's power rather than attenuating it, because the superior is in a position to make the choice. The subordinate, however, cannot step over the line and stand as equal with the superior. The following excerpt comes from a municipal committee meeting. The chair of the committee attends to the positive face of his subordinates by putting them in a one-up position, using a deferential address form in a joking manner, which aims at claiming solidarity with his subordinates.

Example 4.6.   The Committee chair addresses his subordinates, in Cantonese

    1. Chair: *Gwaan1 mun4, gwaan1 mun4,*
                  close door close door TW

2.   *aa1 gam2 do1 wai6 bou6 coeng4 daai6 jan4 aa1.*
TW so many MW department head your-excellency TW

3.   *gam2 jat6 ne1 zau6 hoi1 go3 baan6 gung1 wui6 ji3*
today TW just hold MW business meeting

Close the door. Close the door.
Now, Your Excellencies, the Heads of Departments,
we are going to have a business meeting today.

The chair first directly issues an order to his subordinates ("Close the door. Close the door," line 1), which reflects his power over the addressees (the one sitting next to the door gets up and closes the door). Then the chair uses an archaic, highly deferential form of address, "your excellencies" (line 2), to the same group of addressees. Of course it is not common to use this archaic expression now. The chair uses it in a joking manner to attend to the addressees' positive face, making them feel good by deliberately humbling himself and elevating their status.

But when a subordinate speaks to a superior, he/she tends to use some kind of deference face strategy. In the following example, Yin is talking to his superior, asking for permission to speak. He uses a polite expression *"hou m hou"* (Is it all right?), which reduces the imposition of his request and shows his recognition of the addressee's status.

Example 4.7.   Yin is speaking to his superior

1. Yin: *Hai2, ngo5 nei1 dou3 gong2 gong2 sin1naa4*
yes I here speak speak first TW

2.   *hou2 m4 hou2 ?*
okay not okay
Right, I'll speak first, okay?

In another instance, when Chan, a department head, is talking to his equals, he is also highly deferential on this formal occasion. He makes a request to two other department heads and employs formal expressions to modify his request.

Example 4.8.   Chan to his equals

1. Chan: *Ming4 nin4 jat1 jyut6 jat1 jyut6 zeon2 bei6 on1paai4*
next year January January plan arrange

2.   *gaau2 go3 gim2 caa4 m4 goi1*
make one investigation sorry-to-bother

3.   *dou3 si4 zau6 cing1 zou2 zik1 bou6 tung4*
by time then please personnel department and

4.   *syun1 cyun4 bou6 daai3 jat1 daai3 tau4*
          information department take MW take lead

5.   *fan6 hoi1 saam1 go3 zou2*
          divide into three MW group

          Next January, January, we plan to arrange an investigation.
          Sorry to bother you, but I'd like to ask that the personnel
          department and information department, please take the lead
          and divide into three groups by that time.

Chan uses two polite hedges in his request to his colleagues of the same rank (lines 2 and 3): *mgoi* (sorry to bother you) and *cing* (please). Because this is a formal situation, and Chan is talking to a group of addressees, he tends to be formal and deferential when making the requests. The use of polite hedges indicates his acknowledgment of the situation (an official meeting) and social status of his addressees (equal rank).

These examples show that the use of polite hedges is hierarchical in nature and sensitive to the situation. The speaker tends to be deferential when talking to a superior. But no polite hedge is used when the addressee is a subordinate. The superior has the choice of showing authority over or claiming solidarity with the subordinate. If the speaker is not in a superior position, however, he/she only has one option: recognize the power distance and show deference to the superior. When talking to the equals in a formal situation such as a meeting, the speaker will use face strategies that show deference. If the situation is not a formal one, the speaker tends to use involvement strategies to the equals. This indicates that the speaker is sensitive to the addressee's rank and the type of situation when applying facework. Appropriate linguistic forms are chosen to specify the speaker's acknowledgment of the differences in social status and in situations.

GENDER, AGE, AND RANK IN THE OFFICIAL SETTING

There is always some kind of power difference in interpersonal relationships in any society. Linguistic politeness strategies help to maintain or ratify the power difference. In any face-to-face interaction, it is crucial to recognize the key source of power in that situation and apply the appropriate face strategies. In a society like China, social members tend to see themselves existing in a hierarchical relation to others. Related to this hierarchical relation is the emphasis placed on group harmony. Chinese speakers adjust their linguistic behavior based on the addressee's social attributes such as age, gender, social status and rank, and their relative position (Pan, 1994).

It is apparent from the above analysis that in a Chinese official setting the power derived from a speaker's rank dominates politeness behavior and the choice of face strategies. The speaker's official rank decides his/her position relative to the addressee, which in turn determines what forms should be used linguistically. Speakers have to present themselves appropriately according to their role in the situation. Goffman (1959) points out two aspects of presentational rituals: deference (the appreciation carried by an act, showing regard for the recipient) and demeanor (individuals' ceremonial behavior). In Chinese official settings, deference is shown in one direction, from the lower to the higher level of the power hierarchy. Demeanor requires that everyone behave as is expected of him/her according to his/her social role. A superior should act like a superior, and a subordinate, like a subordinate. Nobody should behave counter to expectation. This Chinese demeanor stems from Confucius' idea that the maintenance of social order depends on every member of society staying in his/her own place in the hierarchy. Though there have been changes since 1949 when the Chinese Communist government came to power and proclaimed equality among people, the deep-rooted hierarchical system is still part of China's tradition and affects the Chinese value system and linguistic behavior today.

Harre and Gillett (1994), when discussing the social psychological sense of self, maintain that to have a sense of self is to have a sense of having a place or places in various manifolds. To understand why Chinese place importance on their relation to each other, we have to understand the Chinese sense of self. In Chinese society, due to the sociocultural tradition of interdependence, people view their connection to others as inevitable. The Chinese concept of self includes the biological individual, his/her immediate environment including family as well as a larger environment including those who are related to him/her either by blood, profession, or locality. In this sense, a Chinese "self" is larger than an individual-centered Western "self" (Hsu, 1981; Zhao & Gao, 1990). Therefore, what is viewed as other persons' individual wants in Western culture may be seen as a shared want in Chinese culture. Accordingly, the desire to be independent and unimpeded in one's actions (negative face) is almost alien to Chinese. It is positive face that is emphasized in Chinese politeness and which explains the subordinate's behavior towards the superior. By showing deference to the superior, the subordinate attends to the superior's positive face want of being recognized and respected as the one who is in a higher position. As for those lower in rank, they do not see themselves as impeded by their superiors for they acknowledge their superiors' right to give direct orders and instructions. An imposition from the superior to the subordinate is not considered a face-threatening act.

In application of politeness rules in the official setting, there is an asymmetrical use of face strategies. The superior can claim camaraderie by following the rule of "be friendly," which is not the case with the subordinate. In a similar manner, the rule of "don't impose" is observed only by the subordinate. The nonreciprocal observation of these politeness rules indicates the recognition of power differences by interlocutors. The speaker's official rank, which is organizational power obtained from the external world, determines whether he/she can impose on others or not.

The power coming from other sources such as age and gender, although very important in Chinese culture, is not recognized to be as crucial as the power source of rank in the official setting. Participants do not show much attention to age and gender differences. Personal connection, which is played out so much in the business setting, is not openly on stage in the official setting. There is no open statement about who is whose friend or who is on good terms with whom. The influence of personal connection is subtly back-staged. In official discourse, the use of personal connection to get things done is currently being criticized as *waifeng* ("crooked wind") and openly condemned. Although everyone knows that personal connection can get oneself entrance into the official world, this kind of negotiation is done with great subtlety and in a private setting (cf. Yang, 1994). Once the setting becomes official, personal connection cannot be openly elaborated. What gets elaborated is official rank. That is why so much attention is paid to the use of face strategies in relation to one's rank position in the workplace.

The situation, however, is quite different if the setting changes. For instance, personal connection is most relevant in the business setting and is the main motivation for the application of facework in service encounters. As I am going to explore in the next chapter, the power associated with gender and age override rank in the family setting. In other words, Chinese speakers adjust themselves to the social constraints imposed by the situation, acknowledging the social contexts of the speech event, and the different power relations in each situation. This constitutes situation-centered and relation-oriented politeness behavior in the Chinese context.

5

"YOU DON'T KNOW WHAT YOU WANT": CONFLICTING FACTORS IN A FAMILY SETTING

In the previous chapter I suggested that once the hurdle of social distance is cleared and participants enter an inside relationship, hierarchical differences become prominent and crucial to the consideration of face strategies. I also demonstrated that in an official setting, the power dimension becomes the primary concern in the choice of linguistic politeness, and power relations are indicated by hierarchical differences in rank. The power that comes with a speaker's rank determines his/her linguistic choices and speaking style in terms of topic-introduction, turn-taking, management of conflict talk, and speech act performance. This suggests that politeness is a dynamic process in which the weight of social distance and power is constantly judged according to the situation and participants constantly adjust face strategies to suit the needs of the situation. The power relationship is constrained and constructed by the social setting in which the interaction takes place. In this chapter, we will look at another social setting, the family gathering, to see how power is structured based on the factors of age and gender.

The family setting is characterized as an informal situation for activities among family members. In this situation intimate relationship is emphasized and the talk is casual, covering a variety of topics, mainly for the purpose of maintaining personal relationships or creating solidarity. Although it is the situation of intimates, there are certain cultural rules governing politeness behavior in a home domain. For example, Blum-Kulka's (1990) cross-cultural study on politeness behavior in Israeli, American, and American immigrant families found that "three key notions combine to set the tone of family politeness: power, informality, and affect" (1990, p. 259). But the perceptions of these three notions and face needs in a family setting are culturally varied. Power relations and display of affect are related to the beliefs and values in a culture. For instance, if hierarchy is of primary concern in a culture, maintaining the power structure will be a key issue in face needs. If display of affection among family members is considered to have high value in a society, then showing intimacy and sharing closeness will be an important face need. It is then essential to look into what constitutes the basic concept of family and the power relations in a family in order to understand politeness behavior within the familial context.

China has traditionally been a highly hierarchical society (Rozman, 1991; Yue, 1989). There is a clear hierarchical order between a relational pair: father-son, husband-wife, older-younger. Within each relational pair, there is one power dimension such as age, gender, or status, that decides who is up and who is down in the hierarchy. A family is the basic unit of this hierarchical structure. A Chinese family is structured on the basis of a patriarchal system, with power descending from the older male to the younger male. Males had absolute power in the traditional family. A woman was part of a man's property and her position in the family was defined from the male perspective. She was supposed to follow "three rules of conduct": before marriage, obey her father; after marriage, obey her husband; and when her husband dies, obey her son. A woman gained status in the family only by giving birth to a boy, and her status increased as she became a grandmother.

When the Communist party took power in China in 1949, one of the significant social changes brought about by the state government was the women's liberation movement. In 1950, a new national marriage law was passed, and for the first time in Chinese history, the law stipulated that a man can have only one wife and that women have equal social status with men (Shen, 1995). Following that, a massive nationwide political campaign to liberate women was carried out. Women were allowed to go to school, to work as equals of men, and to receive the same pay as men for the same job. The Chinese Women's Federation was established as a government organ at every governmental level from national to local government. Its mission is to ensure that, economically and politically, women have equal status and equal rights. More and more Chinese women have received higher education, joined the workforce and become successful professionals in various fields. Nowadays women make up 44 percent of total employment (cf. Min, 1995). Along with these social changes came a change in women's identity and social roles. The traditional role of a woman as a mother and a wife has been challenged. More and more women have started to take up an institutional role and develop a professional identity.

However, these social changes have mainly taken place in the public domain, and were initiated and warranted by the government's administrative measures. In the home domain, traditional practice is preserved because it takes a long time for a social change to penetrate to every sphere of a society. Thus women, especially older and middle-aged women, tend to take the subordinate position to men in a family setting. Another point worth mentioning about the Chinese women's liberation movement is that it was started by the government as a political campaign under the communist ideology of equality. This top-down rather than bottom-up women's movement made most Chinese women passive participants, without much self-motivation or self-awareness, in the government campaign. Thus, conflict arose between the newly built identity of an equal woman and the long-existing traditional expectations for a Chinese woman. I found in my earlier research (Pan, 1996b, 1997a) that while in the workplace official rank gives a woman power equal to that of her male colleagues in politeness behavior, that source of power may be unrecognized, or suppressed in the family situation where traditional values prevail. The power coming from seniority and gender overrides the power associated with rank in language use in the family setting.

These power relations are constructed through language use in family discourse. According to van Dijk (1997), discourse is not only a language activity, but also social action. People engage in various types of interaction such as taking turns, opening and closing dialogues, negotiation, agreeing or disagreeing with each other, responding to previous turns in a conversation, face keeping, being polite, and so on. These verbal activities are accomplished in their social and cultural contexts and are governed by complex rules of social practice in a given situation. This chapter attempts to reveal the social practice of being polite in the context of a Chinese family by observing the verbal interaction among family members of both sexes and different generations.

In order to illustrate my point that discursive features contribute to constructing the power hierarchy among speakers and that a speaker's position in the power structure is perpetuated by language use, I will provide a detailed analysis of one family dinner-table conversation as a case study in the subsequent sections. The family under study is a typical middle class urban[10] family in the city of Foshan, Guangdong Province. The recorded interaction was a New Year's Eve dinner-table conversation lasting about an hour and a half and was conducted mainly in Mandarin Chinese with some segments in Cantonese. The event was video-taped by one of the family members without the presence of the researcher. There were five family members present at the dinner: the mother, the father (who was very sick and was not able to contribute to the conversation), the daughter and her husband, and the son. The mother (Liping) is a retired government official in her late 50s. The daughter (Lanlan) is 35 years old and works as an administrative assistant to the manager of a local branch of the Bank of China. Her husband (Dahua), 40, is the director of a local bank. The son (Jianxin) is 29 years of age and works as the deputy secretary of a municipal government committee. This conversation makes a good study of different sources of power in the home domain because of the age differences and the even distribution of gender among the participants in this case. The social attributes of the participants in age and rank stratum (from high to low) are as follows:

(1) Age hierarchy:mother (Liping, 57)
     son-in-law (Dahua, 40)
     daughter (Lanlan, 35)
     son (Jianxin, 29)
(2) Rank hierarchy: son (Jianxin)
     son-in-law (Dahua),
     daughter (Lanlan)
     mother (Liping)

There are three competing sources of power in this setting: rank,[11] age, and gender. We have seen that in official meetings power coming from one's rank overrides that from age and gender. In the home domain, however, how does the power of rank interact with other sources of power? How do participants position themselves to keep a balance between hierarchy and intimacy so as to achieve harmony among family members? What are the face strategies available to participants to divert possible tension and avoid confrontation in a family setting?

I shall show in this chapter that the significant sources of power in a family setting are the traditional ones of age and gender. Language use by participants in the family setting reflects these dimensions of power, which are embedded in discursive features such as performance of speech acts, topic control, management of conflict, and responses to previous turns. A speaker's linguistic performance and choice of face strategies are a reflection of his/her position in the power hierarchy. The following sections will illustrate the stances taken by participants and the link between gender, age, and rank and the ways in which participants present themselves.

PERFORMANCE OF SPEECH ACTS

Speech acts as a linguistic form have a pragmatic function in interaction. How a speech act is performed depends on the context and the relationship between the speaker and the addressee. Studies (for example, Lii-Shih, 1986; Wierzbicka, 1996) have found that in the Chinese context a more direct way of performing a speech act is preferred in close personal relationships. For example, an imperative (perhaps with some additional "courtesy" phrase comparable to "please") is

TABLE 5.1.   Syntactic Structure of Speech Acts in Family Dinner-Table Conversation

	Speech Acts		
Syntactic structures	Offers	*Requests*	*Summons*
Statement	0	0	4 100%
Basic imperative	5 50%	3 75%	N/A
Question	5 50%	1 25%	N/A
total number	10 100%	4 100%	4 100%

regarded as more appropriate than use quasi-question form. This is because in the Chinese mind a family is the basic social unit with all family members sharing the same interest and functioning as one against the outside world. Within the family, all members are interdependent with one another. An individual self is part of this structure. With this interdependence comes the emphasis on solidarity. But the high degree of solidarity in the Chinese family is structured within the lineage organization of the family, with stress on the young's filial piety to the old and women's subordination to men (Ebrey, 1991). So this kind of solidarity is not based on equality among family members, but rather is hierarchical in nature. Family members position themselves linguistically within this hierarchical structure.

Table 5.1 is a summary of the syntactic structure of the speech acts issued in this interaction. Since this is a dinner-table conversation, speech acts issued consist of three types: offers, requests, and summons, mainly having to do with food serving. The findings confirm Lii-Shih and Wierzbicka's contention that speech acts are performed in a direct way in close personal relationships in Chinese culture. There is no use of politeness hedges or formulaic polite expressions at all in these speech acts.

As the table shows, the basic imperative and the statement are the preferred forms for requests and summons, while offers take the form of imperatives and questions. While it is certainly true that these speech acts are performed without syntactic or lexical modality for politeness purposes, family members use some other linguistic or extra-linguistic features to show hierarchical differences. For instance, if we look at the interactional exchange, we will find that intrinsically polite speech acts (for example, offers, cf. Leech, 1983) are elaborated through several exchanges of turns, and politeness is manifested through interaction, not a single word or expression. Women tend to be more polite toward men. In the following excerpt Liping offers a drink to Dahua, and then both Liping and Dahua ask Lanlan to get the wine and a cup.

Example 5.1.   Making an offer, in Cantonese

> 1. Lip ing: *Jiu3 m jiu3 jam2 bui1 aa1?*
> want not want drink cup TW

Do you want a drink?

2. Dahua: *M jam2. Jau6 mat1je5 jam2 bui1 zau2?*
   no drink have what drink cup wine

   No. Well, what kind of drink do you have?

3. Liping: *Jau6 Gwai3faa1caang4.*
   have Gwai-faa-caang (name of a wine)

   I have Guai-faa-caang (name of a wine).

4. Dahua: *Mou5 hoi1 ge, dou1 mou5 hoi1 dou3 ge.*
   not open TW still not open GW TW

   It's not open yet, not open yet.

5. Liping: *Ei, hoi1 gwo3 ge, go3di1 joeng4 zau2.*
   TW open GW TW those foreign wine

   Oh, it's open. That foreign wine's open.

6. Dahua: *joeng4 zau2.*
   foreign wine

   Foreign wine then.

7. Liping: (to Lanlan)   *Ei, go3, go3 ping4.*
   TW that that bottle

   Okay, that, that bottle.

8. Dahua: (to Lanlan, in Mandarin)
   Na2 ge bei1zi lai2.
   Get a cup come

   Get a cup.

(Lanlan gets up from the table and goes toward the cupboard)

This segment exemplifies a typical offer-acceptance process in Chinese. An offer has to be made more than once before it is accepted. It is considered impolite to accept the first offer, and it is also improper to offer just once. Schiffrin (1994) discusses the essential and preparatory conditions of an offer in four stages: the speaker does not know if the hearer wants A (stage 1), so the speaker finds out if the hearer wants A by requesting information from the hearer (stage 2). When the speaker knows that the hearer wants A (stage 3), the speaker then commits to do A (stage 4). This is why questions can play a critical role in offers: "they reduce uncertainty about whether H wants A, thus, potentially leading to commitment to do A" (1994, p. 74). As we can see from the example, Liping first makes an offer

in a question form (line 1). Dahua's reaction is to decline the offer the first time
(line 2). However he goes on to ask another question about the drink, which
reveals his interest in it. Liping picks up the cue and gives the name of a wine as
a second offer. Dahua's statement in line 4 ("It's not yet open") is his indirect
decline to Liping's second offer, as if he were saying "it is inconvenient to have
the drink since it is not yet open." Liping provides a positive answer (line 5)—this
is her third offer. By then Dahua accepts the offer.

Gu (1990) finds that a successful performance of inviting in the Chinese language takes up an average of three talk exchanges. Of course not every invitation
or offer has to fulfill that requirement. It just indicates a tendency in Chinese culture for the speaker to elaborate his/her assumption about the hearer's wants. The
speaker thinks that an offer or an invitation is a display of generosity and caring for
the addressee. When the addressee makes the initial declination, the speaker has to
insist on issuing the speech act again and again to show his/her sincerity. So the
speaker is doing what the hearer wants: addressing the hearer's positive face. The
exchanges of talk between interlocutors indicate the process of giving and returning positive face to each other. It is then the discourse structure rather than an individual word or use of a single politeness hedge or marker that marks the polite
tone in performing these speech acts.

In contrast, speech acts that place an imposition on the hearer, such as requests,
are performed with a very limited number of talk exchanges. In the above example, Liping asks Lanlan to get the wine (line 7). Lanlan does not give any verbal
acknowledgement to Liping's request. She just gets up and goes toward the cupboard to get the wine. As she is leaving the table, Dahua, her husband, makes
another request of her "get a cup" (line 8). She thus performs the two acts (get the
wine and get the cup) without saying anything. As she returns with the wine and
the cup, neither Liping nor Dahua say a word showing appreciation (like "thanks"
in American English) to her. This is like the closing of the service encounters in
the stamp store discussed in chapter 2.

The underlying reason for this behavioral pattern of elaborating positive politeness in performing speech acts and limiting verbal interaction for speech acts that
are imposing is the emphasis on solidarity in Chinese culture, especially in the
home domain. An elaboration of positive politeness is a show of the speaker's sincerity and solidarity with the hearer. For speech acts that place an imposition on
the hearer, the speaker assumes that the hearer is in a position to perform the act
in terms of ability as well as volition. There is also a shared understanding of one's
relative position to others. For instance, Lanlan is the wife of Dahua and daughter
of Liping. She is expected to perform the duties of a wife and a daughter in the
home domain. Thus Dahua and Liping do not need to redress the face-threatening
imposition of such a speech act, nor is a verbal expression of gratitude expected.
They know their addressee and her position. If they use a formulaic polite expression, that will violate the solidarity rule and create distance between them. As
Wierzbicka (1996) discusses, in Chinese families the message of "autonomy"

would be culturally wrong. Rather, it is important to send to family members a message of unity and interdependence. A characteristic of this kind of politeness can be seen in the taken-for-granted attitude that each family member is doing his/her duty for the good of the family. As a result, speech acts that are potentially face-threatening in Western cultures may not be seen as such in a Chinese family. Directness in performing a speech act creates camaraderie and becomes a display of mutual understanding and solidarity. Because of this, there is hardly any use of politeness hedges or formulaic polite expressions in all my data of conversations among family members.

While solidarity is emphasized in the family setting, hierarchical difference is not ignored. Age and gender subtly affect the use of face strategies among family members. Senior members of the family tend to be more direct and "imposing," while junior members tend to be more deferential towards older members. The senior person, while enjoying higher status, is expected to be benevolent to the young by taking good care of them, and the junior person is expected to show respect and deference to the senior while being taken care of. When age and gender come into conflict, it is gender that overrides age. For example, male speakers use imperatives—a direct way to make requests. A female speaker would use a more indirect way, such as questions, to make requests. In the following example, Lanlan asks her younger brother to help her buy a handbag and her request is turned down by her brother.

> ***Example 5.2.***   Lanlan is making a request to her younger brother
>
> 1. Lanlan: *Shi4 bu4 shi4 ni3 gei3 wo3 mai3 bao1?*
>   Be not be you for me buy bag
>
>   Is it OK to buy me a bag?
>
> 2. Jianxin: *Bu4 gei3 ni3 mai3.*
>   not for you buy
>
> 3.   *Ni3 bu4 zhi1 yao4 mai3 shen2me yang4 de bao1.*
>   you not know want buy what kind GW bag
>
>   **No, I won't.**
>   **You don't know what kind of bag you want.**

Although Lanlan is older than Jianxin, she phrases her request in question form, a less direct and less imposing way of making a request, to speak to her younger brother. But her younger brother's refusal is quite blunt without any face redressive devices. Lanlan does not seem to be offended by Jianxin's blunt refusal, as it is the expected behavior of male speakers. It shows that the performance of speech acts reflects the speaker's position in the family. The directness of a speech act is associated with whether the speaker is a male (in intergender interaction) or

TABLE 5.2. Topic List and Participants in Each Topic

Topics of conversation	Participants in each topic
1. weather	Dahua, Lanlan, Liping
2. making food	Dahua, Lanlan
3. money deposit (for a relative)	Dahua, Liping
4. offering drinks	Liping, Dahua, Lanlan, Jianxin
5. condition of the refrigerator	Dahua, Liping
6. drinks and food (a recurring topic)	Dahua, Liping, Lanlan
7. New Year's visit	Dahua, Jianxin, Liping
8. food market and export	Jianxin, Dahua, Liping, Lanlan
9. food processing	Dahua, Liping, Jianxin
10. inquiry about work	Jianxin, Lanlan, Dahua
11. (code switch) offering food	Liping, Dahua, Jianxin
12. ways of storing liquor	Liping, Dahua, Lanlan, Jianxin
13. clothing fashions	Dahua, Jianxin, Liping
14. celebration of the New Year	Dahua, Jianxin, Liping
15. making deposits at the bank	Jianxin, Dahua,
16. system of foreign checks	Dahua, Liping, Jianxin, Lanlan
17. credit cards	Liping, Dahua, Jianxin, Lanlan
18. ways of making money	Dahua, Jianxin, Liping
19. housework	Dahua, Liping, Lanlan
20. buying medicine	Jianxin, Lanlan
21. weight control	Dahua, Liping, Jianxin
22. tape-recording	Jianxin, Dahua, Liping

whether the speaker is older (in same gender interaction). To act appropriately in this situation means to recognize the importance of this hierarchical structure and the power relations among family members.

TOPIC CONTROL

Sociolinguists use topic analysis to examine the relationship between language use and social factors of power and dominance. Generally speaking, the speaker who introduces the topic in the conversation is most prepared to talk about that subject. Also, the speaker who is given more time to elaborate his/her topic without interruption has the chance to hold the floor longer, and thus dominates the conversation (Shuy, 1982; Wu, 1995). By looking at who introduces conversation topics and how long a speaker holds the floor in a conversation, we can illuminate the power distribution among the participants.

TABLE 5.3. Number of Topics Introduced by Each Participant: $N = 22$

Name	Number	Percentage
Dahua	13	59%
Jianxin	5	23%
Liping	4	18%
Lanlan	0	0%

TABLE 5.4. Number of Topics Each Member Participates In: $N = 22$

Name	Number	Percentage
Dahua	21	95.5%
Jianxin	16	72.7%
Liping	18	81.8%
Lanlan	11	50%

There are several ways to identify a conversation topic. Shuy (1982) combines content definition (clear and uncontestable change of subject focus on what is being discussed) and structural evidence (prosodic devices and internal cohesion devices) for topic introduction or change to identify a topic introduced and discussed in the conversation. Following this definition, 22 different topics are identified in this family dinner-table conversation, and each topic might include several related subtopics. The 22 topics and the number of participants contributing to a topic are presented in Table 5.2. On the left side of the list are the topics being discussed; on the right side are the participants engaged in discussing that topic. The first person appearing in the list for that particular topic is the one that initiates the topic.

Of the 22 topics, only four are introduced by the female group. Liping introduces all four topics (two out of four are simply offering food or drink) while the daughter does not take any initiative at all. The one that introduces most of the topics is the son-in-law, Dahua, who is the oldest male in the group. Although Jianxin is higher than Dahua in the rank hierarchy, he is the youngest of the family. Throughout the conversation, he is less active than Dahua. This is in sharp contrast to the official setting in which Jianxin plays an active part in the official meetings described in chapter 4.[12] In the family setting Jianxin mainly assumes a supportive role to Dahua, but not to the women, as we will see in the following analysis. Table 5.3 is a quantitative summary of Table 5.2.

From the very start, the two men are in a better position to carry on the conversation since they initiate most (82 percent) of the topics. The women, especially the younger one, do not have much chance to contribute to the conversation. The two men not only introduce most of the topics but also participate in the discussion of most of these topics. As for the women, Liping, the mother, takes part in most of the conversation. Lanlan, the daughter, stays away from half of the topics covered in the conversation. Table 5.4 summarizes each member's participation in the conversation.

As Table 5.4 shows the conversation is mainly controlled by the men, particularly by the oldest male in the conversation, Dahua, who is the most active speaker. The next most active speaker is Liping, the mother, and oldest female in the group. The least active speaker is the youngest female, Lanlan, who is not a quiet person by nature. I observed her in other situations such as the workplace and business settings where she is very active. In the workplace she takes a leading role on quite a few occasions when she conducts business meetings and interviews. In the service encounter discussed in chapter 3, she is actively engaged in the conversation with the saleswoman and her friend, initiating the conversation and doing the bargaining. It is obvious that she adjusts her behavior in the home domain to take up the role of a daughter and a wife. The change of situation entails a change of identity and way of speaking. This also indicates that seniority and gender give a speaker the privilege to contribute to conversation in the family. Junior and female members of the family show their respect to senior and male members by being relatively quiet.

As the conversation is dominated by men, when a woman tries to get the floor, she usually runs into obstacles and has to face two options: one is to keep trying; the other is to drop her intention of getting the floor. Following are two examples showing how the women try to get the floor.

Example 5.3.   When talking about drinks

Dahua: *Jin1 nian2 zhong1guo2 nian2 he1 yang2 jiu3*
this year Chinese (new) year drink foreign wine

This year we have foreign wine for the Chinese New Year.

2. Liping: *Yang2 jiu2?*
foreign wine

Foreign wine?

3. Jianxin: *Zhei4 jiu3 yi1ban1hua4.*
this wine so-so

This wine is just so-so.

4. Liping: *Nei4 zhong3 shi4 shen2me pai2 a? Wo3 gao3 bu4 qing1chu3*
that kind is what brand TW I know not clear

What brand is that? I'm just not familiar with it.

5. Lanlan: *Zuo2tian1 yi1xia4zi ...*

yesterday all-at-once

Yesterday, all at once …

6. Liping: *You3de chen2 jiu3, chen2 jiu3 fang4 duo1shao3*
some old wine old wine store how-many

7. *nian3 dou1 bu1 pa4 de a.*
years still not afraid-(of-going-bad) GW TW

Some old wine, old wine, even if stored for many years, it's still good.

8. Dahua: *Kai1 de bu4 xing2.*
open GW not good

Once opened, it goes bad.

9. Lanlan: *Na4 ni3 hai2 you3 shi1du4, wen1du4 shi4 duo1shao3*
well you also have humidity temperature be how-much

Well, it also depends on the humidity and temperature.

10. Dahua: *Kai1 de, kai1 le ping2 zen3me dou1 bu4 xing2*
open GW open GW bottle how still not good

Once opened, if the bottle is opened, no matter what, it's no good.

In the above example, Dahua introduces the topic of foreign wine (line 1). Then Jianxin and Liping join him in discussing the topic. In line 5, Lanlan intends to start something new and changes the topic by talking about what happened the day before. The change is indicated by the time referent "yesterday," which gives a different time frame than the current one, and the phrase "*yixiazi*" (all at once). In Chinese, the phrase "*yixiazi*" is a counter word for a verb—a description of an action, which is certainly not related to the "wine" topic. But she is cut off by Liping in line 6, who continues the topic of foreign wine introduced by Dahua. Then Lanlan drops her topic initiation and joins her husband's topic of wine in line 9.

If a woman intends to continue with the attempt to introduce her topic, she has to keep trying or wait for another chance. In the following example Liping's topic is interrupted by male speakers, and she has to make another try to get the floor.

Example 5.4. When talking about fashion

1. Liping: *Na4, Mei4mei4 na4 nian3 …*
that Meimei that year …

That, that year, Meimei …

2. Jianxin: *Ta1men zuo4 xi1zhuang1 qu4 Nanhai zuo4 xi1zhuan1*
    they make western-suit go Nanhai make western-suit

    When they have western-style suits made, they go to Nanhai city.

3. Dahua: *Na4 ge, Pingzhou na4 ge.*
    that one Pingzhou that one

    That one (tailor), the one in Pingzhou (town).

    (Conversation goes on for three minutes)

4. Liping: *Shang4 ci4 Xiao3dong1 dao4 Bei3jing1*
    last time Xiaodong go Beijing

5.   *bu4shi4 gei3 Mei4mei4 yi1 jian4 qiu2mao3 ma ...*
    isn't give Meimei one MW fur-coat TW

6.   *Fan3zheng4 shi4 bi3jiao4 gao1 dang3 le. Zai4 Bei3jing1 mai3 de,*
    anyway be relatively high class TW in Beijing buy GW

7.   *cai2 liu4 bai3 duo1 kuai4 qian2 la, hai2shi4 duo1shao3 qian2.*
    only six hundred over MW money TW or how-much money

    Last time when Xiaodong went to Beijing,
    didn't he buy a fur coat for Meimei?
    Anyway it's relatively high class. Bought in Beijing,
    Just over six hundred yuan (Chinese dollars), or something like that.

8. Jianxin: *Dao4 guo2wai4 jiu4 gao1 ji2 le.*
    go abroad then high class GW

    Well, it looks high class once you take it abroad.

In this example, Liping tries to give a narration of what happened that year (line 1), but is interrupted by her son, who then initiates his topic of making western-style suits. Dahua responds to Jianxin's remark rather than to Liping's. Liping has no choice but to join the men's topic. The conversation goes on around the topic of making western-style suits for three minutes. Then Liping tries again to bring up her topic (line 4). She gets the floor this time and gives a short narrative of the event (Xiaodong bought a fur coat for Meimei).

The relatively subordinate position of the women is indicated in control of the conversation. While the men get the floor naturally and easily, the women very often have to try hard to get their voices heard. In the above two examples, Lanlan, who is junior in terms of age, simply withdraws from trying since all her addressees have more power (through either gender or age). She is left very little chance of getting the floor. Liping, who is in a relatively higher position because of age seniority, has to make a special effort and try a second time before she can get the floor. When her topic is cut off she has to wait for three minutes until Jianxin and Dahua finish talking about the topic of making western-style suits, and only then does she pick up her original topic. If a woman is persistent in pursuing her topic introduction, she is seen as violating the politeness norm in the family domain, because a woman is expected to put herself in a lower position than men in the hierarchical system at home. In the case cited above, family harmony is preserved when a woman knows how to step aside and support male speakers in the conversation.

POSITIVE RESPONSES TO MEN'S TALK

How conversation participants respond to previous turns or prepare next turns frames the position of the previous speaker. Thus responses as a discursive feature can indicate the speaker's perception of power relations in a conversation. Responses to the points under discussion made by the previous speaker can be positive or negative. By positive, I mean such utterances as reinforcement, agreement, and elaboration of the points made by the previous speaker. Positive feedback elevates the importance of the issue and encourages the discussion. In contrast, negative responses include distancing, disagreement, doubt, refusal and denial. In general, a negative response downplays the issue and may discourage the speaker from continuing the topic if he/she cannot respond to the challenge.

There are noticeable differences in the way participants respond to points made by a man or a woman in the home domain. In this conversation the participants of both genders mostly respond favorably to issues raised by the men, particularly Dahua, since he is the oldest male in the group. In other words, the authoritative position of men is not only indicated by the number of topics they introduce, but also by the way participants respond to their talk. On the other hand, the participants, especially the men, are not as enthusiastic about the points made by the women. They often neglect or refute the females' points, or show disagreement and doubt. Though the two women tend to support each other, their fragile "female alliance" often falls into pieces when confronted with powerful male superiority.

In the following two excerpts, the participants show positive responses to the points made by the oldest male speaker, Dahua. These responses include active participation, showing agreement, and giving elaboration and details. In Example 5.5, Jianxin and Liping are quite interested in Dahua's topic of setting up a joint-venture poultry processing plant. They actively join him in the discussion.

Example 5.5.   Dahua brings up the topic of the possibility and difficulty of setting up a joint-venture poultry processing plant. Jianxin and Liping participate in the discussion.

1. Dahua: (Cantonese) *ji5hau6 dou1 hai6 wan2 zyun1 jan4*
           later all be find special person

2.   *lei4 tong1 gai1 saai1 aap3, gam2 ...*
    to kill chicken kill duck, so ...

3.   (Mandarin) *Ben3lai2 zhei4ge jin4cheng2 ying1gai1 kuai4 de*
          actually this process should quick GW

4.   *Zhong1guo2 na4me duo1 ren2li4. Zhe4, zhei4 ge wan4yi1*
    China so much manpower this this MW thing

5.   *yi1 nong4 qi3lai2 jiu4 gao3 gan1jing4, shi4 ba.*
    as-soon-as set up then make clean be TW

    (Cantonese)
    (You) should find someone who specializes in killing and cleaning chickens and ducks, so ...
    (Mandarin)
    Actually this process could be speeded up.
    China has so much manpower.
    Once this, this thing was set up,
    it would be quite easy to do the cleaning, right?

6. Jianxin: *M*
    TW

    Yeah.

7. Liping: *Jiu4 hao3 guo3 ni3 zi4ji3 ge4 jia1 ge4 hu4*
    just better than you self each family each household

8.   *qu4 gao3 ma. Ta1 ji2zhong1 gao3 ne,*
    go do TW it concentrate do TW

9.   *ta1 zuo4wei2 yi1 zhong3 gong1zuo4, ta1 you4 wu2 suo3we4i de a*
    it as a kind job it also no matter GW TW

10.   *Ru2guo3 wo3 sha1 ge ya1zi,*
    if I kill MW duck

11.   *wo3 jiu4 guang1 shi4 na4 dao4 gong1xu4.*
    I then only be that MW process

12.   *Wo3 ye3 you3 gong1ju4 you3 shen2me,*
    I also have tool have what

13.   *wo3 jiu4 bu4hui4 fan2 le. Zuo4wei2 yi1 ge4 jia1ting2,*
                 I then won't frustrated GW. As a MW family

14.   *you4 yao4 zhei4 yang4 you4 yao4 na4 yang4.*
                 also need this kind also need that kind.

It would be better than doing it yourself in your own house.
If it was done in an organized way,
it would be taken as a kind of job,
then it would be no big deal.
If I kill ducks, I'm only responsible for one process.
I also have the tools or whatever.
Then I won't be frustrated.
But at home, you need this and that …

15. Jianxin: *Kai1 ge4 tu2zai3chang3 bu4 shi4 na4me rong2yi4 kai1 de,*
                 open MW slaughterhouse not be so easy open GW

16.   *Wu1ran3 hen3 da4, na4xie1 xue3.*
                 pollution very big that blood

17.   *Yuan2lai2 zai4 Daliang shi2 da3suan gao3 yi1 ge4.*
                 originally in Daliang when plan set-up one MW

18.   *Yi1 tian1 zai3 bu4 zhi1dao4 duo1shao3 wan4 zhi1 ji1,*
                 one day kill not know how-many ten-thousand MW chicken

19.   *na4 ge4 tu2zai3chang3 …*
                 that MW slaughterhouse

To open up a poultry slaughterhouse is not so easy.
There's a lot of pollution, so much blood!
Originally I planned to set up one in Daliang County.
It could kill, I don't know how many thousands of chickens in
one day.
Oh, that slaughterhouse …

20. Dahua: *Wo3men2 bu4 zhi1 you3 mei2 you3 na4me duo1 ji1 lai2 xian1.*
                 we not know have not have so many chicken come first

We don't know if we have that many chickens.

21. Jianxin: *Ren2jia jiu4 shuo1 ni3 you3 mei2 you3 na4me duo1 ji1 ya1,*
                 they just say you have not have so many chicken TW

22.   *yao4 sha1 liang3 qian1wan4 dun1 ji1 cai2 gou4.*
                 need kill two ten-million ton chicken then enough

23.   *Liang3 qian1wan4 dun1 ji1 shi4 deng3yu2 duo1shao3.*
             two ten-million ton chicken be equal how-many

24.   *Yao4 duo1shao3 hu4 ren2jia lai2*
              need how-many household family come

25.   *yang3 zhei4 ge4 ji1 gong1chang3, shi4 ba*
             support this MW chicken plant be TW

             Yeah, people ask whether you have that many chickens.
             You would need to kill twenty million tons of chickens,
             How much is twenty million tons of chickens equal to!
             Well, how many families specialized in raising chickens
             would the plant need? Right?

26. Liping: *Ni3 ke3yi3 gao3 xiao3 xing2 yi1dian3 de ma.*
             you can set-up small type little GW TW

             Well, you could set up a smaller one.

27. Dahua: *Ta1 na4ge4 dong1xi xiao3 xiang2 yi3hou4 ne, ta1 ...*
             it that thing small type after TW, it

             If it was a small one, it ...

28. Jianxin: *Mei2 xiao4yi4 de.*
             no profit GW

             Wouldn't make any profit.

29. Dahua: *Mei2 xiao4yi4.*
             no profit

             Wouldn't make any profit.

30. Jianxin: *Mei2 xiao4yi4. Suo3yi3 ren2jia1 wei4shen2me*
             no profit therefore people why

31.   *neng2gou4 ba3 qi3ye4 quan2li4 dou1 na2 hui2qu4.*
             can take enterprise rights all take back

             Wouldn't make any profit. That's why the foreign partners
             would take back the enterprise ownership.

The topic of opening a poultry processing plant is initiated by Dahua (lines
3–5). Jianxin and Liping show interest in the topic and give their own opinions. Liping emphasizes the convenience of a poultry processing plant and
provides details and examples (lines 7-14). However, Jianxin looks at the

other side of the coin: the problem of pollution and the amount of supply the plant would need (lines 15-19). Dahua reinforces Jianxin's point by saying that they would be short of supply (of chickens, line 20). Jianxin then develops Dahua's point and gives details about the amount of supply needed (lines 21-25). When Liping comes up with the alternative of setting up a smaller plant, the two men do not seem to like the idea. The opposing opinion is introduced by an if-clause ("If it was a small one, it …") in Dahua's utterance (line 27) and completed by Jianxin in line 28. All this indicates that the participants (except Lanlan who keeps silent during most of the conversation) are actively engaged in the topic, giving analysis and opinions. Their involvement in the topic elevates the importance of the issue raised by the men.

Following is another example of a positive response to men's talk in which the participants respond favorably to the point made by Dahua by showing agreement and giving elaboration.

Example 5.6.   Talking about clothing fashions

1. Dahua: *Jin1 nian2 guo4 chun1 jie2 man3 jie1 dou1 shi4 hei1 de*
this year observe spring festival full street all be black GW

2.   *dou1 shi4 pi2 jia2ke4 hei1bu4liu1qiu1 quan2bu4 ren2*
leather jacket black-ugly all people all be

3.   *dou1 shi4 chuan1 zhao1pai2, zui4 nan2kan4.*
all be wear brand-name most ugly

This Spring Festival the whole street is filled with black.
Everybody's wearing leather jackets, black and ugly.
Everybody is after the brand name, so ugly!

4. Liping: *Na4xie1 ren2 dou1 shi4 yi1 chang3 feng1.*
those people all be one MW fashion

Those people are after the fashion.

5. Dahua: *Ren2ren2 dou1 you3 yi1 jian4.*
everybody all have one MW

Everybody has one.

6. Liping: *Na4 zhei4 yang4 ne bian4 de qian1 pian1 yi1 lu4,*
then this way TW become GW thousand article one pattern

7.   *mei2 yi4si le.*
not interesting GW

That way, everybody looks the same. It's dull.

8. Dahua: *Mei2 yi4si, fan3zheng4 yi1 yan3 kan4 guo4qu4.*
not interesting anyway one look see over

9. *Wo3 zui4, zui4 ming2xian3 chu1yi1 de shi2hou4*
I most most obvious New-Year-Day GW time

10. *wo3 kai1 che1 chu1qu4, zai4 Fo2shan1 shi4 shang4*
I drive car out in Foshan city on

11. *zou3 liang3 bian1, shi4 rong2 hen3 hao3kan4,*
go both side city scenery very nice

12. *zhong1jian1 yi1 tiao2 xian4 hei1 de*
middle one MW line dark GW

It's dull when you see it, anyway … I, most …
It was most obvious when I went out driving on New Year's Day.
When you go around the city of Foshan,
the scenery on both sides of the street is very nice,
but in the middle there is a black line (of people wearing
black jackets).

13. Liping: *Ha, ha …*
(laughter)

14. Dahua: *Hei1hu1hu1 de, nan2 de ye3 shi4 hei1 de,*
black GW man GW also be black GW

15. *nyu3 de ye3 shi4 hei1 de.*
women GW also be black GW

All are black. Men are in black and women are in black, too.

16. Jianxin: *Na4 ge4 pi2 yi1 hen3 gui4 de.*
MW leather coat very expensive GW that

17.   *Na4 tian1 liang3 qian1 ba1 bai2 duo1 kuai4...*
that day two thousand eight hundred more dollars

That kind of leather jacket is very expensive.
That day, two thousand and eight hundred dollars …

18. Dahua: *Suo3yi3 Zhong1guo2ren2 xi3huan1 gan3 chao2liu2.*
so Chinese like catch fashion

So Chinese like to follow the fashion.

19. Liping: *Shi4 ya, shen2me dong1xi dou1 xi3huan1gan3chao2liu2,*
right TW whatever things all like catch fashion

20.   *yi1 wo1 feng1.*
             one hive bee

             Right, like to follow the fashion, no matter what, just like a hive
             of bees.

21. Jianxin: *Bu4guo4 ne, ta1jie1shang4na4xie1hen3duo1 dou1shi4*
             but TW it street on those very many all be

22.   *jia3 de pi Pi2 j ia2ke4.*
             fake GW leather jacket

             But many of them in the street are just wearing fake leather
             jackets.

Dahua brings up the subject of the current fashion and shows his resentment of it (by calling it "black and ugly"). His resentment finds an echo in the statement of Liping, who concludes that the fashion is dull (lines 6-7). In the following turn, this comment is repeated by Dahua, who continues to elaborate his argument, giving more specific information and an example (lines 8-12). The remark made by Jianxin in lines 16-17 is also in support of Dahua, providing details about the cost of leather jackets. When Dahua draws the generalization (line 18) that Chinese like to follow fashion, Liping reinforces his conclusion by giving a metaphor, "just like a hive of bees" (lines 19-20). Jianxin's statement in lines 21-22 stresses the same point: people are so concerned with fashion that they will even wear fake items to appear fashionable.

As illustrated above, participants react actively to topics brought up by the men. Positive responses in this talk consist of repeating the same information, expressing the same opinions and making contributions to the topic under discussion by giving information and providing examples. This is a way of showing politeness to the man who introduces the topic, making him feel his viewpoint is valued and shared by all—his positive face want is satisfied. In the Chinese way of thinking, the opinions of those who are in an authoritative position are considered as important enough to be valued. In the family setting, men, especially those who are senior in age, are conventionally believed to be in an authoritative position and thus their talk deserves more attention. As we are going to see in the following section, responses to the women's remarks often convey a negative tone of downplaying, denial, or refusal. Gender is obviously a key factor in politeness behavior in the home domain.

Dahua is older than Jianxin, but lower in rank. Even though Jianxin's official rank is higher, Jianxin mainly assumes a supportive role of Dahua. This is indicated by the fact that Dahua initiates most of the topics and Jianxin usually shows agreement with what Dahua says. This shows that age seniority is the deciding power for one's position in the family within the same gender group.

TABLE 5.5. Question-Answer Pattern for Each
Participant in Family Dinner-Table Conversation

Questions asked by	# of questions	Questions answered		Not answered	
		#	%	#	%
Liping	28	15	54 %	13	46 %
Lanlan	4	4	100 %	0	0
Dahua	27	27	100 %	0	0
Jianxin	13	11	85 %	2	15 %

NEGATIVE RESPONSES TO WOMEN'S TALK

While the men's utterances receive positive feedback, there is a general tendency to downplay what the women say. Due to the low status of Chinese women in the past, women's talk in intergender interactions is traditionally viewed as negative. The Chinese language has many expressions representing this negative view concerning women's speech, for example, "When three women are together, they can perform an opera" (*san ge nyuren yi ta xi),* meaning women are always loud and noisy, and talking nonsense); "Long hair, but short knowledge" (*toufa chang, jianshi duan)*, indicating that what a woman says should not be taken seriously; "A long-tongued woman" (*chang she fu*), meaning women frequently gossip. These linguistic expressions embed a cultural belief that women's speech is trivial and is unworthy of attention. They have also become metaphors for women's speech. Although Chinese women's status has been undergoing tremendous changes in the past 50 years due to the government campaign for women's liberation, the deep-rooted negative view of women's talk still exists in today's language behavior. Especially in the family setting, where traditional values dominate, women are supposed to be in a subordinate position to men. While men's talk is taken seriously by the participants, women's talk is downplayed. In this section we will see how the participants react to the women's talk. Two features show this point. One is the question-answer pattern of how participants pick up the questions raised during the conversation. The other is negative responses to women's talk, which include disagreement, doubt, refusal, or denial. As a whole, negative responses downplay the issue and may discourage the speaker from continuing her topic.

Question-Answer Pattern

A clear feature of negative response to women's talk is that throughout conversation men's questions are answered in almost every case, but women's are very often ignored. Asking questions during a conversation can just indicate one's interest or involvement and not all questions require an answer (Tannen, 1984), but the fact that there is a great difference between the number of answers to the questions raised by male speakers and female speakers indicates something about the general attitudes toward male and female speakers in the conversation. Table 5.5 shows the number of questions, including requests for information, confirmation and clarification, asked by each participant and the response to these questions by other participants.

As the table shows, most of the male speakers' questions are answered. Being the oldest male in the conversation, Dahua has his questions answered in every case. Jianxin, the youngest in the group, has most of his questions answered with only two questions ignored by the group (15 percent of the total number of questions asked). As for female speakers, though Lanlan's questions are answered in every case, we have to take into the consideration that the number of questions she asked (just four) is by far the smallest of all the participants. She almost has no chance to ask questions. Liping, the mother, has nearly half of her questions (46 percent) ignored by the participants. The absence of answers to Liping's questions indicates a lack of attention from the participants. Liping might have raised questions to show her interest in the conversation, but her questions are quite often brushed aside. The following example shows how Liping's question is ignored while Jianxin's gets an answer.

> ***Example 5.7.*** When talking about a check sent by Meimei (Liping's younger daughter) from America to Liping
>
> 1. Liping: *Qian1 ming2 shi4 Mei3mei de qian1ming2 ba?*
> sign name be Meimei GW signature QW
>
> 2. *Hai2shi4 Xiao3dong1 de qian1ming2?*
> or Xiaodong GW signature
>
> Is it (the check) signed by Meimei or by Xiaodong?
>
> 3. Jianxin: *Qian1ming2 bu4 hui4 na4me yuan3 qu4 dui4,*
> Signature not can so far go match
>
> 4. *dui4 bu4 liao3 de ba?*
> match not possible GW QW
>
> Is it possible to check the signature from so far away? It's not possible, right?
>
> 5. Dahua: *Chuan2zhen1 guo4 lai2 de.*
> fax over come GW
>
> It's sent over by fax.
>
> 6. Jianxin: *Chuan2zhen1 guo4 lai2.*
> fax over come
>
> Oh, by fax.

In this excerpt, both Liping and Jianxin ask Dahua (who is the director of a bank) questions concerning a check sent from America. Since Liping does not know English, she cannot read the signature on the check. So she asks a question about the signature (line 1). Jianxin's question seeks more information on the signature: how to check if the signature is real (line 3). Dahua readily answers Jianxin's question ("It's sent by fax," line 5) and not Liping's, though Liping's question can be considered a pre-condition for Jianxin's question about how to check the signature. Liping's question in the end is still left unanswered.

Instances of this do suggest that the women's questions are not taken as seriously as the men's. Furthermore, Liping does not persist in asking the question again if it goes unanswered. But Jianxin, the youngest in the family, whose questions sometimes are not answered immediately, states the question again to get an answer. This may have to do with the way the men and the women view themselves. Since the Chinese family is based on patriarchal authority and female subordination (Luo, 1996), Chinese women are taught to accept their subordinate position when talking to male family members at home. Thus, Liping does not mind that her questions are neglected by the others. This is not the case with Jianxin.

Downplay of Women's Remarks

Another type of negative response is to downplay the importance of a woman's utterance. Refusal and disagreement are two typical strategies to display negative feedback to the previous speaker. The following two excerpts (Example 5.8 and 5.9) exemplify the negative responses female speakers receive during the conversation.

Example 5.8.   Lanlan is making a request

1. Jianxin: *Hou4tian1 hai2 yao4 qu4 ci4 san1 shui3*
the-day-after-tomorrow again need go once Sanshui

2.   *Hou4tian1 qu4 ci4 Sanshui*
the-day-after-tomorrow go once Sanshui

I have to go to Sanshui (town) again the day after tomorrow.
Go to Sanshui the day after tomorrow.

3. Lanlan: *Shi4 bu4 shi4 ni3 gei3 wo3 mai3 bao1?*
Be not be you for me buy bag

Is it OK to buy me a bag?

4. Jianxin: *Bu4 gei3 ni3 mai3. Ni3 bu4 zhi1 yao4 mai3 shen2me yang4 de bao1.*
not for you buy you not know want buy what kind GW bag

No, I won't. You don't know what kind of bag you want.

5. Liping: *Shen2me bao1, shou3ti2bao1 a?*
                what bag handbag TW

                What kind of bag? A handbag?

6. Dahua: *Shen2me dong1xi dou1 ke3yi3 bang1 ni3 mai3,*
                what thing all can help you buy

7.   *shou3ti2bao1 shi4 mei2 na3 yi1ge4 bang1 ni3 mai3.*
                handbag be no which one help you buy

                He could buy anything else for you.
                But nobody can help you buy a handbag.

8. Jianxin: *Mei2you3 ban4fa3 bang1 ni3 mai3.*
                no way help you buy

                There is no way I can help you buy it.

9. Dahua: *Ei4, shou3ti2bao1 yi1ding4 yao4 zi4ji3 mai3*
                TW handbag definitely need self buy

                Yeah, you definitely have to buy a handbag yourself.

In this excerpt Lanlan makes a request asking her younger brother, Jianxin, to buy her a handbag (line 3). Her request is structured in the form of a question, which reduces the imposition of the request and thus makes it more polite (Brown & Levinson, 1987). But Jianxin not only refuses her bluntly without any face-redressive device ("No, I won't," line 4), but also implies that Lanlan is the one that is to blame since she does not know what she wants. He repeats his refusal in line 8 ("There is no way I can help you buy it"), leaving Lanlan no space to negotiate. Interestingly, Dahua, her husband, joins Jianxin, reaffirming and giving an explanation for Jianxin's refusal (lines 6–7, and line 9) rather than taking his wife's side.

The following excerpt is a continuation of the above conversation. When Liping sees that Lanlan's request has been turned down by Jianxin, she tries to suggest a compromise, forming some kind of alliance with her daughter. Liping also receives a negative response.

Example 5.9.   Liping suggests an alternative

1. Liping: *Sanshui de mao3yi1 luo.*
                Sanshui GW sweater TW

                How about a sweater from Sanshui?

2. Jianxin: *Sanshui de mao3yi1 you3 shen2me hao3.*
                Sanshui GW sweater have what good

                What's so good about Sanshui's sweaters?

3. Liping: *Ei2 Sanshui de mao3yi1 you3ming2 de, shen2me mei2 sha2 ming2*
TW Sanshui GW sweater famous GW what no what name

Oh, Sanshui's sweaters are famous.
Why do you say they are not?

4. Jianxin: *Gaoming cai2 you3.*
Gaoming only have

Only Gaoming (town) has (sweaters).

5. Dahua: *Gaoming*
Gaoming

Gaoming.

6. Liping: *Gaoming ye3 you3, Sanshui ye3 you3.*
Gaoming also have Sanshui also have

Gaoming has sweaters, but Sanshui does too.

7. Lanlan: *Sanshui ye3 you3ming2.*
Sanshui also famous

And Sanshui's are famous.

8. Dahua: *Xian4zai4 dao4chu4 dou1 shuo1 ta1 you3ming2.*
now everywhere all say it famous

9.   *Ni3 ye3 bu4 zhi1dao4 ting1 shei2 de fan3zhen4shi4*
you also not know listen who GW anyway

These days, everybody everywhere claims to be famous.
You don't know who to trust, anyway.

Liping, seeing that her daughter's request has been refused, suggests an alternative (to buy a sweater from Sanshui, line 1). Jianxin's statement "What's so good about Sanshui's sweaters" (line 2) is another way of saying "I'm not going to buy the sweater either." Liping tries again, saying that Sanshui's sweaters are famous (line 3). Jianxin denies her proposition and says that "Only Gaoming has sweaters," implying Liping does not know the situation. Liping defends her position (line 6), and Lanlan shows support for her (line 7). But Dahua's last utterance denies the validity of their claims, thus refuting the women's defense ("These days, everybody everywhere claims to be famous. You don't know who to trust, anyway," lines 8–9).

The above two examples indicate that gender is the main concern in choosing the type of response to a previous speaker. While the male's points are applauded by all, the importance of a female speaker's argument is often minimized. The female speakers are discouraged from elaborating their ideas, and are often confronted with a negative response: neglect, disagreement, and downplay, particularly from the male speakers. Thus, responses, as an interactional strategy, also encode face concern for power differentiation based on gender and age in the home domain.

MEN AND WOMEN IN CONFLICT TALK

Conflict is often viewed as negative in Chinese culture and emphasis has been made on how to preserve harmony and avoid conflict in interpersonal relationships. Within the hierarchical face system in Chinese society, conflict resolution depends on maintenance of harmonious face relations, and on the power relation as well. Face has literal meaning in that the individual must be able to face associates and accept hierarchical differences without rancor (Scollon & Pan, forthcoming). I suggested in chapter 4 that there is a clear power distribution in the use of opposition strategies in conflict talk in the official setting and that power derives from one's official rank. In the family setting, we have different dimensions of power: gender and age. Conflict is managed along these two power dimensions. That is, when conflict occurs, speakers choose linguistic strategies that signal the recognition of gender and age differences. Harmony is achieved by participants' careful alignment with their allocated right to speak in the hierarchical structure.

Teams in a Conflict

A special characteristic of the management of conflict talk is that when an argument occurs the men and women form two separate teams. The opposition turns are not just between two opposing conversants; instead, they are between two teams: the men's team and the women's team. The two men give mutual support to each other, while disagreeing with the women. The two women usually stand by each other, but as the conflict goes on, they change their positions by either dropping their opinion or taking up the role of mediator. A female speaker is more likely to encounter disagreement from other participants than a male speaker, and the oldest male is least likely to be challenged. It is often the case that the conflict is resolved with the female speakers giving up pursuit of their argument and accepting the male speaker's position.

In the following excerpt, the four participants are arguing about the counterfeit trademark on some canned food. Lanlan is warning the family members that they should be careful about canned food because there is a lot of fake stuff on the market. The two men show obvious disagreement with her warning. Liping first sides with Lanlan. Later, she downplays Lanlan's point and takes up the role of mediator.

Example 5.10.   Talking about the counterfeit trade mark on some canned fish

1. Lanlan: *Wo3 ting1 guang3bo1 jiang3 le, chu2le Guang3zhou1*
I hear broadcast say GW except Guangzhou

2.   *shi4 zheng4zong1 de, ge4 di1 lie4 chu1lai2,*
be genuine GW every place list out

Shun4de2 Gui4zhou1, gao3bu4hao3 ...
Shunde Guizhou very-likely

I saw on TV that except for Guangzhou, all the places listed,
such as Shunde, Guizhou, very likely ...

3. Liping: *Jia3 huo4 a?*
fake goods TW

Fake stuff?

4. Lanlan: *Ei4.*
yeah

Yeah.

5. Jianxin: *Gui4zhou1 shi4 mao4pai2 huo4. Zhei4 ge4 yu2 bu4 shi4.*
Guizhou be fake goods this MW fish not be

The sfuff from Guizhou is fake. But this fish isn't.

6. Lanlan: *M4*
TW

Um

7. Jianxin: *Ta1 zhei4 ge4 guan4tou2 chang3 shi4 ding4dian3 chang3
lai2 de.*
it this MW can-food factory be state-designated factory come
GW

This canned food factory is designated by the state.

8. Dahua: *Ta1 neng2gou4 da3 Zhu1jiang1 pai2 de ne ...*
it can use Zhujiang brand GW TW

If it can use the brand name of Zhujiang ...

9. Jianxin: *Jiu4 shi4 zheng4pai2.*
Then be real

Then it's real.

10. Dahua: *Jiu4 shi4 zheng4pai2.*
               Then be real

               Then it's real.

11. Jianxin: *Ta1 jiu4 shi4 na4 ge4 Zhu1jiang1 pai2 de*
               it just be that MW Zhujiang brand GW

12.   *na4 ge4 ding4dian3 chang3 lai2 de ma.*
               that MW state-designated factory GW GW tw

               It's just that the Zhujiang factory brand is designated by the
               state.

13. Lanlan: *Bu4 shi4. Ta1 na4 tian1 bo1 ...*
               not be it that day broadcast

               No, that day the TV said ...

14. Liping: *Na4 zhao1pai2zhi dou1 ke3yi3 mao4 de*
               that brand-label all can fake GW

               Even the brand label can be fake.

15. Lanlan: *Ta1 xian4zai4 zhuan1men2 bo1 chu1lai2,*
               it now special broadcast out

16.   *shuo1 na4 xie1 chang3 mao4 pai2, ma1de,*
               say which ones factory fake brand damn

17.   *xian4zai4 chu2le Guang3zhou1 na4 ge4 shi4*
               now except Guangzhou that GW be

18.   *zheng4zong1 de, qi2ta1 quan2 dou1 shi4 mao4 pai2 de*
               genuine GW others all all be fake brand GW

19.   *Ya1, na4 tian1 dian4shi4 zhuan1men2 jie4shao4*
               TW that day TV special introduce

20.   *zhei4 ge4 jie2mu4. Suo3yi3 wo3 di4er4 tian1*
               this MW program so I second day

21.   *gei3 ba4ba mai3 de shi2hou4 jiu4 te4bie2 zhu4yi4*
               for father buy GW time then special attention

22.   *kan4 shi4 bu4 shi4 mao4 paiz de.*
               see be not be fake GW

               There was special program on TV telling people
               which factories use fake brand labels. Damn,
               now, except for the real one in Guangzhou,

they're all using fake brand labels.
Ah, that day, the TV ran a special program on this.
So the second day when I bought it (the canned fish) for father,
I paid special attention to see if it was fake.

23. Liping: *Bu4 pa4, jiu4 ba3 ta1 zheng1 guo4,*
             not afraid just with it steam GW

24.   *ye3 hao3 guo4 zi4ji3 zhu3wa*
             also good GW oneself cook tw

             Don't worry. Just steam it.
             It's still better than cooking it yourself.

25. Dahua: *Hao3 guo4 zi4ji3 sha1 yu2 ma.*
             Good GW oneself kill fish tw

             Better than killing the fish yourself.

26. Liping: *Shi4 a, hao3 guo4 zi4ji3 sha1 yu2 ma.*
             right TW good GW oneself kill fish tw

             Right, better than killing the fish yourself.

             (pause for 20 seconds)

There are three points that I want to make about the above example: first, is how the speakers express their opposition; second, is the solidarity each speaker displays toward the one in the same gender group; and, third, is Liping's shift of position from an opposing party to a mediator.

First, Lanlan makes the point that there is quite a lot of canned fish imitating a famous brand on the market and that they should take the problem seriously (lines 1–2). To back up her point, she cites a TV program as the source of her information (TV programs are considered as having authoritative value in China). However, she immediately encounters opposition from the male speakers. Jianxin first gives a partial agreement in line 5 ("The stuff from Guizhou is fake.") and then uses the word "but" to introduce disagreement ("but this fish isn't"). Lanlan does not agree with Jianxin, but she does not explicitly state it. She just makes a nasal sound indicating her doubt (line 6). In contrast, Jianxin explicitly expresses his opposition, giving details on what kind of factory produced the canned fish (line 7). Dahua shows his agreement with Jianxin in line 8 and 10. Lanlan then uses a stronger opposition word "no" to start again and tries to fight back by giving more detailed information on the TV program that warned people of the fake brand products (lines 15–22). By now the argument is getting tense with the males directly opposing Lanlan, and Lanlan trying to defend her position.

Second, speakers of the same gender group support each other. Ellipsis and repetition are two techniques speakers use to display their solidarity.[13] Interestingly, a female speaker fills in or repeats the other female speaker's utterance while a male speaker does the same for the other male speaker. The repetition and ellipsis is never cross-gender. The instances where ellipsis and repetition occur are presented again as follows.

I.

    1. Lanlan: *Wo3 ting1 guang3bo1 jiang3 le, chu2le Guang3zhou1*
          I hear broadcast say GW except Guangzhou

    2.   *shi4 zheng4zong1 de, ge4 di1 lie4 chu1lai2, Shunde*
          be genuine GW every place list out Shun4de2

          Guizhou, gao3bu4hao3 …
          Gui4zhou1 very-likely

          I saw on the TV that except for Guangzhou, all the places listed, such as Shunde, Guizhou, very likely …

    3. Liping: *Jia3 huo4 a?*
          fake goods TW

          Fake stuff?

    4. Lanlan: *Ei4.*
          yeah

          Yeah.

II.

    13. Lanlan:*Bu4 shi4. Ta1 na4 tian1 bo1 …*
          not be it that day broadcast

          No, that day the TV said …

    14. Liping: *Na4 zhao1pai2zhi dou1 ke3yi3 mou4 de*
          that brand-label all can fake GW

          Even the brand label can be fake.

In these two instances, Lanlan uses ellipsis in her turns, and Liping completes Lanlan's sentences by filling in the deleted information. This ellipsis and information filling is a display of understanding and high involvement (Tannen's term, 1986) between the two women. Okazaki's (1994) study also indicates that ellipsis is a frequently used strategy to show intimacy and involvement in the Japanese language.

The two male speakers use the same strategies of ellipsis and repetition to support each other in this argument. The following is an instance of the two males supporting each other by ellipsis and repetition.

III.

> 8. Dahua: *Ta1 neng2gou4 da3 Zhu1jiang1 pai2 de ne ...*
> it can use Zhujiang brand GW TW
> If it can use the brand name of Zhujiang ...

> 9. Jianxin: *Jiu4 shi4 zheng4pai2.*
> Then be real
> Then it's real.

> 10. Dahua: *Jiu4 shi4 zheng4pai2.*
> Then be real
> Then it's real.

In this instance, Dahua's utterance is not complete, but Jianxin joins him in finishing the sentence. Jianxin's involvement can be seen as showing his eagerness to render support to Dahua's point. Then Dahua repeats what Jianxin says. This also indicates the two men's solidarity in the conflict talk.

Third, Liping is at first on the same side as Lanlan. However, seeing that the conflict is getting tense, Liping changes her position and takes up the role of mediator. She starts to downplay the importance of Lanlan's argument, saying that the issue of fake canned food is not significant and that there is still something good about the fake canned fish ("better than cooking it yourself," line 23). Dahua gives another reason for not taking the warning seriously ("Better than killing the fish yourself," line 24), and Liping repeats Dahua's statement. This repetition indicates the shift of Liping's stance from an opposing party to a mediator, which is the signal of her attempt to avoid further argument and resolve the conflict. At this point, Lanlan does not say a word, and the issue is dismissed.

It could be argued that Lanlan is opposed by the men because she does not have age seniority. However, Liping, the oldest female in the group, does not fare much better, as shown in the example below.

Example 5.11.   Talking about the best way to store wine

> 1. Jianxin: *Zui4hao3 shi4 zai4 na4ge4 tong3 li3mian4*
> best be in that MW barrel inside
>
> The best way is to store it in a barrel.

> 2. Dahua: *M4*
> TW
>
> Um.

> 3. Liping: *Zhuan1men2 cheng2 jiu3 de tong3 a?*
> special contain wine gw barrel tw
>
> In a barrel specially made for storing wine?

4. Jianxin: *Ei4.*
              TW

              Yeah.

5. Liping: *Tong3 hai2 bu4 hao3. Wo3men2 zhong1guo2*
              barrel still not good we China that

6.   *na4ge tan2 a, na4ge4 tao2ci2 zhuang1xia4 ...*
              that MW jug TW that porcelain contain

              A barrel is no good. Our Chinese jugs, those porcelain jugs
              can contain ...

7. Jianxin: *Ren2jia1, ren2jia1 zuo4 na4ge4 tong3 ...*
              people people make that MW barrel

              People, people make that barrel ...

8. Dahua: *jiu4 yao4 na4ge4 tong3 de wei4, na4ge4 mu4tou2 de*
              wei4dao4.
              just need that barrel GW flavor that wood GW flavor

              To have the flavor of the barrel, the flavor of wood.

9. Jianxin: *Jiu4shi4 ta1 na4ge4 mu4tou2 lai2 bian4 yan2se4 ma, ni3*
              zhi1dao4 ma?
              Just it that wood to change color tw you know TW

              The wood changes the color (of the wine), y'know.

10. Dahua: *Dui4 a.*
              right TW

              That's right!

11. Liping: *A, yao4 mu4tou2?*
              TW need wood

              What? It has to be wood?

12. Dahua: *Gang1 bu4 xing2 de.*
              Jar not do GW

              A jar won't do.

13. Liping: *Yao4 mu4tou2 a?*
              need wood TW

              It has to be wood?

14. Dahua: *Ei4, ta1 na4ge4 mu4tou2 shi4 zhuan1men2 shen2me zang2?*
              TW it that wood be special what store

15.   *mu4 zuo4 chu1lai2 de jiu3 jiu4 you3 shen2me wei4,*
             wood make out GW wine then have what flavor

16.   *ji2shi3 ta1 shen2me mu4 niang4 chu1lai2 jiu3,*
             actually it what wood make out wine

17.   *niang4 chu1lai2 jiu3 jiu4 shen2me wei4.*
             make out wine then what flavor

             Yeah. That kind of wood is special for storing wine.
             The wine will have the flavor of the wood it's stored in.
             Actually the wine will have the flavor of the wood that you use
             to make it, to make the wine.

18. Liping: *Ei4.*
             TW

             Eh.

19. Dahua: *Zhe4 yang4 de.*
             this way GW

             That's the way.

20. Liping: *Ei2, xian4zai4 wo3men2 na4ge4 yi3jing1 shi4 lu4 zhe de a ?*
             TW now we that already be record GW GW TW

             Oh, our conversation is being recorded now, isn't it?

21. Lanlan: *Dui4 a.*
             right TW

             That's right.

22. Liping: *Ei4, lai2, gan1bei1, gan1bei1.*
             TW come cheers cheers.

             Oh, come on. Cheers, cheers.

When talking about the best way to store wine, Liping disagrees with Jianxin's
statement. At first, she does not openly state her disagreement, instead, she just
shows her doubt by asking a question (line 3). In line 5, she explicitly states her disagreement and gives her opinion on the best way to store wine (in a Chinese jug).
But before she can finish her sentence, Jianxin cuts off her argument and Dahua
sides with him by continuing Jianxin's sentence. Liping is left in the minority.
Faced the opposition, Liping just repeatedly asks the same question "Has to be
wood?" and does not pursue it any further. When Dahua finishes his reasoning, Liping quickly changes the subject (line 20) and completely abandons the conflict talk.
Also she realizes that their conversation is being recorded, and it may be embar-
rassing to show disagreement on tape. So she gives a toast to make everyone happy.

Termination of a Conflict

Vuchinich (1990) analyzes multiple instances of conflict talk occurring during family dinners and aims to determine both the different ways in which conflicts are ended and the frequencies of different termination modes. He reports five termination formats: submission, dominant third-party intervention, compromise, withdrawal, and stand-off. As many scholars have pointed out, Chinese culture places a high value on group harmony and avoidance of conflict. Conflict is resolved through either compromise or mediation (Hwang, 1997). In the Chinese family gathering under study, there are five instances of conflict talk occurring during the conversation. The two most common modes of conflict termination are withdrawal and third-party intervention. There is a tendency for women to withdraw from the conflict. Of the five arguments, two are terminated by the women's withdrawal, two ended with a mediator (once by Liping and once by Dahua) initiating compromise and giving "face" to both parties, and one reaches a consensus after a few exchanges of opposing turns. On average, there are just two rounds of exchanges of opposition turns between the opposing parties and then the conflict is terminated.

The one that functions as the mediator is either Liping or Dahua, both older speakers in the group. The example where Dahua functions as a mediator is found in their argument about which town has sweaters. The men say Gaoming and the women say Sanshui.

Example 5.12.   Liping suggests that Jianxin buy Sanshui's sweater for Lanlan

1. Liping: *Sanshui de mao3yi1 luo.*
Sanshui GW sweater TW

How about a sweater from Sanshui?

2. Jianxin: *Sanshui de mao3yi1 you3 shen2me hao3.*
Sanshui GW sweater have what good

What's so good about Sanshui's sweaters?

3. Liping: *Ei2, Sanshui de mao3yi1 you3ming2 de,*
TW Sanshui GW sweater famous GW

4.   *shen2me mei2 sha2 ming2*
what no what name

Oh, Sanshui's sweaters are famous.
Why do you say they are not?

5. Jianxin: *Gaoming cai2 you3.*
Gaoming only have

Only Gaoming (town) has (sweaters).

6. Dahua: *Gaoming*
Gaoming

Gaoming.

7. Liping: *Gaoming ye3 you3, Sanshui ye3 you3.*
Gaoming also have Sanshui also have

Gaoming has sweaters, but Sanshui does too.

8. Lanlan: *Sanshui ye3 you3ming2.*
Sanshui also famous

And Sanshui's are famous.

9. Dahua: *Xian4zai4 dao4chu4 dou1 shuo1 ta1 you3ming2.*
now everywhere all say it famous

10.   *Ni3 ye3 bu4 zhi1dao4 ting1 shei2 de, fan3zhen4shi4*
You also not know listen who GW anyway…

These days, everybody everywhere claims to be famous.
You don't know who to trust, anyway…

The two men agree that only Gaoming has sweaters, and the women believe Sanshui has the best sweaters. There are two rounds of exchange of opposition turns between the major opposing parties. Jianxin's opposition turns are in lines 2 and 5; and Liping's in lines 3 and 7, with Dahua giving Jianxin support in line 6 and Lanlan supporting Liping in line 8. After each speaker has stated his/her own view, Dahua takes up the role of mediator in his last elliptical statement (lines 9-10), which is an indirect way of saying that since we don't know who to trust, let's forget about the issue.

Argument as a form of discourse can be used to achieve certain social goals in some cultures. For example, in the Jewish American community, argument is used as a means of sociability among group members and as a way to train children to become members of the community (Schiffrin, 1984). In the Chinese context, however, argument is generally avoided especially when there are hierarchical differences (of rank, gender, or age) between the participants. To be polite is to keep harmony and to recognize the hierarchical position each participant occupies. Open confrontation among hierarchically differing participants is seen as a challenge to the hierarchy, and very rude. Since harmony is the expected norm in the Chinese behavioral pattern, an individual's opinion, compared with group harmony, is insignificant. Group harmony is thus achieved with each participant acting according to his/her role in the situation.

SETTINGS AND POWER RELATIONS

In this chapter, gender, age, and rank are discussed in relation to the use of face strategies in a family setting. While each factor definitely affects politeness behavior, it is interesting to note how they give way to one another within a particular situation. In the home domain, by Chinese tradition, the younger should show filial piety to the older, and women be subordinate to men. The Confucian idea is that when this order is maintained, everyone can live in harmony (Yue, 1989). This ideological belief is embedded in the face system and reflected in politeness behavior at home.

The use of face strategies is closely associated with the perception of interpersonal relations in a discourse system, and politeness means appropriateness to the perceived relationship and the situation. Since gender and age are perceived as important dimensions in the hierarchical structure in the home domain, speakers choose face strategies that signal the recognition of these differences. Junior members of the family use language in a way that shows respect to senior member by complying with requests, avoiding disagreement, and being deferential. Female speakers, even if senior in age, tend to assume a subordinate position to male speakers in their employment of linguistic politeness, for instance, by showing support to men's talk, following men's topics, avoiding conflict, and phrasing speech acts in a more indirect way. Face strategies used by women in the conversation are a reflection of social practice and social expectations of the role of women in the home domain.

In public domain interactions such as service encounters and official meetings, gender is not perceived as a crucial power dimension. Age is considered important only when other factors are equal. In service encounters, *guanxi* (personal connection) is the main factor that triggers the application of facework in verbal interaction. In the workplace, women, when allowed by their ranking positions, do not act as mere subordinates to men. Rather those lower in rank take the subordinate role regardless of gender. In other words, there are different social requirements for politeness practices in various situations, and speakers constantly adjust their roles and speaking strategies to fit the social expectation imposed upon the individual in a particular situation.

When comparing American and Chinese behavior, Hsu (1981) maintains that Chinese tend to be situation-centered and Americans tend to be individual-centered. That is, situation places more serious restrictions on Chinese behavior in contrast to American individual-centered behavior, in which the self-imposed norm plays a more important role in behavior. In the individual-centered culture, if an individual's behavior is inconsistent across situations, he/she will experience inner conflict, because this is seen as breaching one's moral standards and integrity. Therefore, politeness behavior is more a matter of individual choice, while in the situation-centered pattern of behavior, an individual is always seen in relation to others. His/her behavior should be consistent with the social requirements of the situation, including acknowledgment of power relations and recognition of situational variation. Because of this, consideration of how one is related to others in terms of hierarchical difference and calculation of others' wants are the basic rules for appropriate behavior. Failure to follow these expectations incurs serious face loss, damage to personal connections, and threat to group cohesion. In this way, politeness places a social sanction on individuals in Chinese culture (Gu, 1990), and minimizes an individual's inner face need.

To a point of view that does not recognize the pattern of identifying the important elements in a situation, determining the sources of power and hierarchical order among the participants, and applying politeness strategies accordingly, Chinese may seem to be erratic in their politeness behavior and have flexible rules for practice in different settings. This may also be the reason why Chinese are seen as inscrutable by Westerners. If we understand the underlying motivations of politeness practice in Chinese culture, we will be able to resolve the apparent inconsistency of politeness behavior in different situations in the Chinese context.

6

"WHAT REALLY IS CHINESE POLITENESS?" A SITUATION-BASED APPROACH TO POLITENESS

"Tell me really what Chinese politeness is in one simple sentence," a U.S. diplomat studying Chinese at the Foreign Service Institute asked me upon learning that I had been doing research on Chinese politeness behavior, "so that I can remember it and know how to deal with the Chinese when I'm in China." I found it hard to give him a satisfactory answer.

It is difficult for two reasons. One is because of the different assumptions held by people in different cultures about how to be polite. The other is because of the multiplicity of politeness behavior in a particular culture. I will take up these points one at a time.

The first point concerns the cultural values associated with the assumptions about politeness in different cultures. My student's question presupposes the American view that a person has a stable character and will act the same way and use the same politeness strategies in whatever situation he/she finds him/herself.

However, the foregoing analyses of politeness behavior in the three settings of service encounters, official meetings, and family gatherings in Southern China show that Chinese seem to have a very flexible way of being polite. Chinese will act according to the situation they are in, and use different politeness strategies depending on the social relationship. Therefore, face systems as cultural tools are used differently to mediate social interaction among participants in sales encounters, in business meetings, and in family dinners. In service encounters the relationship is primary. Among strangers in state-run businesses, there is little facework. In private enterprise, salespersons attend to the face of potential customers by cultivating relationship. In a business meeting, relationship and hierarchy determine whose speech is most authoritative. Within this setting, rank is more important than gender. At family dinners, however, gender is more important than rank, with a male having more say than his wife, sisters, and even his mother. This situational variation in Chinese politeness behavior makes it hard to give a clear-cut definition of the Chinese way of being polite.

Actually the approach to the problem of politeness is different in each culture. Earlier in this book I mentioned anthropologist Francis Hsu's description of Chinese culture as situation-based in contrast to America's individual-centered culture. As reflected in politeness behavior, this contrast leads Chinese to use polite strategies depending on whether they are necessary in a particular social relation and a particular situation, while Americans use politeness strategies out of respect for the other individual, regardless of who the addressee is. But to Chinese, the addressee's social attributes of rank, age, and gender are crucial factors influencing the choice of politeness strategies. During one of my lectures in China, a Chinese student asked me: "Why are Americans so polite, always saying 'please,' and 'thank you,' even to their family members? To me, Americans are hypocritical because it is not necessary to say these all the time." This Chinese student's question is based on Chinese assumptions about politeness. That is, you use polite strategies in certain situations where it is required by the social norm to act politely and where there are obvious power differences. That is why Chinese are often seen by Americans as inconsistent in their behavior. Many of my foreign service students working in China have commented on this inconsistent behavior of their Chinese colleagues. They can be very polite and deferential in one situation, but quite impolite in another.

The second point that I want to discuss is the multiplicity of politeness. To understand politeness in Chinese culture, we need to understand first that there are situational variations in politeness behavior, and different sources of power are recognized in each situation. Secondly, there is multiplicity in politeness behavior in a particular culture. Politeness behavior as social practice has multiple aspects. There is not just one general idea, nor is there one single dimension applicable across all situations that dominates politeness behavior in a particular culture. Rather it is multidimensional in that there are multiple factors involved in the consideration of facework. It is difficult to decide which dimension is most essential

TABLE 6.1. Settings and Social Factors

	Rank	Age	Gender	Connection
Business setting	–	–	–	+
Official setting	+	+/-	–	–
Family setting	–	+/-	+	–

in determining the choice of face strategies, because each dimension plays its role differently depending on environment, and each factor is part of the combination in a larger context. We should not neglect contextual constraints on the function of each dimension. If we draw any conclusion about cultural characteristics based on one dimension, it will be quite misleading because social variables vary even within one single culture.

Let us consider the interaction of setting and social factors in Chinese politeness behavior. The preceding discussion on politeness in three settings in Southern China shows that the four social factors of rank, age, gender, and connection do not share equal weight across settings. They override each other in the consideration of face strategies. Table 6.1 shows which factor has a significant role (marked with +) in a specific situation. The one marked with +/– (for example, age in official and family settings) means the factor is significant under certain conditions. For instance, age is significant in the official setting when other factors are equal, and in the family setting when within the same gender group.

Here the relative importance of each social factor depends upon the situation in which interaction takes place. Otherwise, it is easy to overemphasize one factor and neglect the others. To take the factor of connection, for example, while it is generally believed that *guanxi* is of primary importance in Chinese culture, its role in the application of facework is limited to the business setting. Of course, this is not to say that connection does not have an affect in other situations, it is just to say that connection has a key function at the entrance into the inner circle of social relationship. Once inside the circle, other social factors take over. Within the inner circle, official rank overrides age and gender in the workplace, and gender overrides rank and age in a family situation. Age plays a role in both the workplace and the family domain only when other factors are equal. This runs counter to the popular belief that age seniority gives a person high status in Chinese society.

So while it is tempting for us to draw conclusions about Chinese characteristics for purposes of cross-cultural comparison, it is truly impossible to do so without knowing what social setting we are talking about. If we start with consideration of the situation and then go on to explore how sociological variables function in the defined situation, we have a more concrete base for exploring cultural differences.

Let us first look into the variable of social distance. In the Chinese context, there is a large social distance between ingroup and outgroup members. The social boundary of inside and outside relations is so clearly marked that it has become an index for the application of politeness strategies. But acquaintance with someone's acquaintance can easily close that distance. This is because *guanxi* has primary importance in daily life, and people try, whenever possible, to build new connections and extend their old ones. Acquaintance with somebody else is the first introduction to the new network. As reflected in language use, people are friendlier toward their acquaintances and use linguistic strategies that emphasize connection and closeness. On the other hand, with outsiders, the use of facework is very limited. In some cultures the distinction of inside and outside relationship may not be that crucial in social interaction. Then the role of social distance in the consideration of face strategies is less significant.

Almost all studies on politeness discuss the importance of power relations, but it is crucial to recognize what confers power in a given situation, be it rank, age, gender, or social status. In some cultures, for example, India or Colombia, social class is a crucial factor in determining power hierarchy. In this book, I have shown that connection, rank, gender, and age are the basic determinants of the power structure for the consideration of face strategies in contemporary China, but that the role of each factor varies according to the specific situation. These social factors may be suppressed in one situation but played up in another. As is shown in the previous chapters, the importance of rank is recognized in the official setting, but suppressed in other situations such as service encounters and the home domain. Gender is suppressed in professional discourse, but played up in the family situation.

The multiplicity of politeness lies also in the fact that politeness as a social practice is influenced by historical development in a society and that politeness behavior should be viewed from a historic perspective. Politeness behavior encodes reaction to and reflection of social and historical developments, political environment, and economic changes. In situations like service encounters, it is clear that economic reforms in China brought about the change in politeness behavior from being task-oriented to being connection-oriented. The overriding power of rank in the official setting reflects the traditional value attached to official rank as well as the political system of contemporary China. In the family situation, a microcosm of the long-existing social model in China, the patriarchal system continues to dominate. The traditional practice of showing deference to the older male is maintained in this setting, while with the open-door policy since the early 1980s, there was a big wave of western influence in the public domain affecting the use of polite expressions. All of these historical influences and social developments are interwoven in politeness phenomena in contemporary China. If we do not look at the evolution of politeness phenomena in relation to social change, we will miss some very important clues as to why there are various ways of being polite.

What this means is that politeness is a dynamic process which involves the participants' perceptions of social distance, context, and power relations in face-to-face interaction. The weighting of these variables is governed by social practice and ideology in a given culture. In order to avoid binarism and cultural stereotyping, we need to examine not only the relationship between linguistic politeness and social variables but also how each of the social variables functions in a specific situation, what face strategies are used to address these variables, and how politeness practice reflects social practice in a culture. Only then can we expound cultural differences and draw comparisons across cultures.

POLITENESS AS SOCIAL PRACTICE

In Brown and Levinson's (1987) politeness model, the notion of face is claimed to be universal, because it is based upon a rationalized individual's psychological needs. Many studies have contested the universality of face and challenged the individual-based approach to politeness. In the foregoing discussion, I suggested that politeness behavior mirrors social organization and power relations ingrained in a society, which is part of the cultural knowledge that social members acquire through the socialization processes. So politeness is not only an individual's face want, but also a social practice and reaction to power relations defined in a society. Politeness is a social practice because politeness behavior is the ideology of how human relationships are perceived and how an individual is related to others in a certain cultural context.

In Chinese society, an individual self includes intimate associates, thus being a more widely circumscribed self, while Americans draw a boundary between the individual's expressive conscious and his or her intimate associates (Hsu, 1981). For Chinese group boundaries are more important while for Americans the individual face need is more basic. This difference in boundaries implies different relational nuclei with different face strategies, with mitigation of face threat less important where group boundaries are relatively permanent than where the individual is paramount (Scollon & Pan, forthcoming). Thus, the notion of negative face want (to be independent of others) applies more to the relational nuclei whose boundaries focus upon each individual. The positive face want of being the same as others is more pertinent to the group-oriented culture where sharing and mutual dependence are emphasized. So the notion of face need is intimately associated with the cultural value placed upon human relations.

Positive face want can be said to be the basis for politeness practice in Chinese culture. Sameness and oneness (*dayitong*) have been the paramount ideal sociopolitical order in Chinese history (Zhao & Gao, 1990). There is also a strong need to be part of a group, be it a family or a social circle. An individual is perceived as in coexistence and in a dyad relation with other social members. The dyadic relation binds individuals into a social network of mutual dependence. Therefore, the desired face strategies in face-to-face interaction are those that reinforce the bonding between group members and enhance the face need of being liked and being the same. Positive politeness satisfies this kind of face need and is favored in interaction among Chinese. It reflects the social

Situation → What setting is this?

Social distance → What social
relationship is this? Inside or outside?

Power relation → What power relation
is recognized in this setting?

Source of power → What is important in
the power relation? Is it age, gender,
rank, social class?

FIGURE 6.1.

practice of emphasizing ingroup cohesion and solidarity among group members. But solidarity is emphasized under the condition that the hierarchical order is maintained. I call this hierarchical solidarity: hierarchical because solidarity is not based on equality among group members but on the power structure established in the society. Each social member acts according to his/her role as defined by the situation. When the hierarchical order is institutionalized and becomes stable, solidarity is then the main focus.

The social practice of using politeness strategies to address the hierarchical order and solidarity when engaging in face-to-face interaction among Chinese follows certain steps. There are four basic questions to consider in the application of facework in a given situation as shown in Figure 6.1.

Thus, there are at least four dimensions governing the choice of linguistic politeness. When you are in a particular setting, which is more or less bounded, you define the situation, then define the social relationship. Once you are in the inside circle, the power relationship becomes important. Then you have to decide what source of power is recognized in the particular setting, and apply face strategies accordingly. The steps involved are as follows:

1. identification of social relationship
2. recognition of hierarchical order
3. identification of power source
4. application of facework to attend to the social relation and the power hierarchy

The first step is to measure the social distance between the two participants. Is it an inside relation or an outside relation? Are they in the same system? This social distance not only determines the type of social relations they are in, but also the linguistic strategies applied to address the need to interact with other social members. For an outside relationship, the concern of face is irrelevant because participants do not know each other's relative position in the social hierarchy. Information about the addressee's social attributes of rank, age, and social status is not available to the participants in an outside relationship. It is, therefore, impossible to place each other in the hierarchical structure and use face strategies accordingly. As we noticed in the previous chapters, the imposition of a face-threatening act (FTA) is a linguistic feature free of social context, while the addressee's social attributes are context-sensitive. Face strategies in Chinese face-to-face interaction are used to address power differences and to attend to the addressee's social attributes, but are not necessarily used to reduce the imposition of an FTA. In other words, social factors take precedence over linguistic factors in face consideration. This is why an outside relationship does not require face strategies; the social attributes of both participants are not present, and thus not relevant. What is relevant to the situation is the social distance perceived by the participants and the intention of both parties to reduce the distance or maintain it at that level.

The need to reduce social distance can be pragmatic or instrumental. In a business setting, for example, there may be no pre-existing inside relationship. But when the need arises to attend to face concerns so as to attract customers and do business, people have to apply face strategies. The first step is to break the ice by reducing the social distance and placing each other in the hierarchical system. This is done by asking about background information such as personal history and social connections and claiming connections with each other. It is important to understand how this inside system functions and works. It places participants in an invisible network of connection and hierarchy. Within this system, face is mutually granted and enhanced. Once outside this system, face is no longer an issue because people do not see the need to apply face strategies. In this sense, linguistic politeness is not so much determined by the imposition of an FTA as by the social distance between the speakers. In a society where social distance is not treated as that crucial, for instance, in American society, the imposition of a single speech act carries more weight. That is, whether in an intimate relationship or a distant one, speakers use linguistic politeness to modify the imposition of a speech act if it is deemed as face-threatening. Studies have found that English speakers use the quasi-question form to make requests to addressees in both close and distant relationships (for example, Wierzbicka, 1991, 1996). That is because requests are deemed as face-threatening and need to be modified by linguistic means to reduce the imposition to the individual regardless of the type of social relation. But in Chinese culture, the social practice is to determine the type of relation first and then to use politeness strategies accordingly.

The second step in the application of face strategies is to recognize the power difference and acknowledge the hierarchical order between participants. This power relation is extremely important for interaction in an inside relation in which participants are obliged to acknowledge the social stratification and power differences among the group members who share a sense of mutual dependence. This mutual dependence comes from the practice that the person in the superordinate position is in some way obliged to take care of and cultivate the person in the subordinate position, and in turn, receives respect and deference from the subordinate. The subordinate, while giving deference to the superordinate, receives protection and benevolence from the superordinate. They mutually benefit from the hierarchical structure and from the interdependence among group members. Face strategies as cultural tools are used to ratify this hierarchical structure existing in an inside relation. For example, the superordinate will use involvement strategies to "speak down" to the subordinate, while the subordinate will employ face strategies that show deference and respect to "speak up" to the superordinate.

The third step is to identify the source of power in a specific situation. The power that the addressee possesses (from age, gender, or rank position) is the key determinant of the use of politeness strategies by the speaker. The speaker tends to modify his/her speech according to whom is being spoken to and the situation. If the addressee is lower in status than the speaker, no facework is needed. It should be noted, however, that in different settings, different sources of power are acknowledged.

So face strategies are indeed linguistic features attending to the social relationship and power structure. These differential power structures are part of social organization and social members learn how to be part of that organization, and how to deal with power relations when engaging in social interaction. This is the socialization process that members of a cultural group have to go through in order to become full members of the community. Each culture has its own definition of what is important in social organization and social members learn the face system that attends to it.

In describing how *guanxi* (personal connection) is produced in Chinese society, Kipnis (1997) outlines the complexity of gift exchange, visit exchange and favor exchange in daily life in a Northern Chinese village. During these seemingly complex exchanges, villagers socialize themselves to become fellow members of a community and create a bond, that is, *guanxi* network, with each other. (This is very much like a Japanese practice. See Nakane, 1970; Yamada, 1997). While doing this, they also acquire the face strategies that enhance this bonding. If an individual is socialized in a different cultural context, he/she will learn a different system of facework that meets the needs of the given social environment. For instance, a Chinese born and growing up in the United States will certainly acquire a different way of being polite from a Chinese born and socialized in China. For the former, individual face need will be of primary importance, while for the latter, the group and social bonding will be the main concern in the choice of face strategies.

POLITENESS AT THE DISCURSIVE LEVEL

Linguistic politeness has been studied mostly at the level of a single speech act such as apologies (for example, Fraser, 1981; Olshtain & Cohen, 1983; Trosborg, 1987), directives (for example, Ervin-Tripp, 1976; Pufahl, 1986), compliments (for example, Manes 1983; Wolfson, 1993), requests (for example, Blum-Kulka, 1987; Clark & Schunk, 1980; Zhang, 1995), invitations (for example, Wolfson, D'Amico-Reisner, & Huber, 1983), and so on. Comparisons have been made across cultures to contrast the linguistic realization of politeness in these speech acts and to identify cultural values associated with linguistic politeness. In this book, I have argued that politeness is realized not only at the level of syntax and lexical items, but also at the level of discourse. That is to say, a variety of discursive elements in verbal interaction have the function of attending to face needs and work as face strategies in verbal interaction.

Linguistic features under study are of two levels: speech acts and discourse structures. On the level of speech acts, I mainly focused on the performative speech acts of directives, requests/compliances, and offers with regard to their syntactic structures and lexical items that express politeness (politeness markers). I found that the majority of speech acts are issued without syntactical or lexical modalities that express politeness. When speakers do employ politeness markers in issuing a speech act, it is only in limited situations that politeness markers are used, such as in the official setting when the addressee is in a superordinate position or is a group of people, and sometimes in the business setting when the speaker is a female or a teenager. In other words, the use of politeness markers in the performance of speech acts is mainly for emphasizing the formality of the occasion, for example, an official setting, and not so much for the purpose of mitigating the imposition of a speech act. Formulaic polite expressions or politeness markers are not used frequently even in a friendly encounter. Under normal circumstances, it is discourse structures/strategies that cue people's politeness behavior in the Chinese context.

This is why I have conducted a detailed examination of discourse structures in the course of my discussion, which includes the opening/closing of an interaction, length of the interaction, management of conflict talk, the decision-making process, small talk, code-switching, topic control, responses to previous turns, and question-answer patterns. It is at the discourse level that the major social factors—age, gender, ingroup identity, and official rank—influence politeness behavior. What makes an interaction polite and friendly are the discursive features that permeate the interaction. They are the prominent features in the verbal interaction which signify face strategies at the discourse level.

Some features are present in all three settings, and this is thus possible to compare them. Following is a summary of linguistic features across settings:

1. *Directives* are mostly issued in a direct way, using a flat statement or imperative. Formulaic polite expressions or politeness hedges are not often used with directives. Their usage is mainly found in the official setting and in the private store in the business setting. Offers and invitations are also issued without politeness markers, but have to be completed through a few turn exchanges to show politeness.
2. There are very limited verbal expressions in *responses to directives* (either orders or requests). The addressee usually performs the act requested by the speaker without verbal acknowledgment. This behavior is consistent across the three settings.
3. *The management of conflict talk* is similar in the official and the family setting in that the one highest in the hierarchy has the final say. But in the family setting, the exchange of opposition turns is very limited, whereas in the official setting argument can be longer and the directness of expressing opposition is linked with rank, not gender. Means of terminating an argument are also different. In the official setting, argument is usually terminated by the person with the highest rank, while in the family conversation it is ended either by a mediator or by the women's withdrawal.
4. *Conversation topics* are largely controlled by the person highest in rank in the official setting and by male speakers in intergender conversation in the family setting. Furthermore, participants respond positively to males' speech and negatively to females' speech. In the official setting, however, gender differences are not as obvious as rank differences in the use of politeness strategies.
5. *Small talk* has an important function in building connection and is employed often in the business setting and the workplace.

The fact that politeness is signaled more at the discourse level poses some important questions for us to consider, such as how to investigate politeness phenomena, how to teach each language and culture in the second language classroom, and how to conduct intercultural training. It is relatively simple to carry out comparative studies on speech acts and polite expressions across languages and cultures, because speech acts and polite expressions are relatively easy to define and identify. It is also relatively easy to teach politeness behavior at this level. When politeness is viewed at the discourse level, however, it forces us to go beyond the clear-cut definition of a set phrase of politeness and to look for new ways to identify face strategies. However, I believe this is a significant step in furthering the study of politeness phenomena. It will bring us to the next level of comparison and a deeper understanding of politeness behavior as a social practice. It will also yield a richer result in cross-cultural study and intercultural training. Most miscommunication occurs not at the level of syntax or a single speech act, but at the level of discourse, such as how to open a conversation, how to respond to a previous turn, how to introduce a topic, and so on. Understanding politeness practice at the discourse level will enable us to become aware of cultural preferences in signaling how to be polite in verbal interaction. It will also help us to develop a broader framework for analyzing politeness across cultures.

In the age of the information superhighway, it is tempting to look for short and simple explanations for cultural differences in politeness behavior, but they often by-pass the complexities involved in the communication process. In this book, I have tried to explain the cultural variables that are involved in politeness practice in Chinese culture and how they come together in the hope that it will shed light on the understanding of politeness phenomena in a larger social context.

Notes

---

1. Though addressed to the servant, it is meant to be heard by the guest, a typical way of doing things in those days. Otherwise it would be unnecessary to be so polite to the servant.

2. MW = measure word throughout the examples.

3. TW = tone word throughout the examples.

4. QW= question word throughout the examples.

5. GW = grammar word (including particle, possessive, tense and aspect marker) throughout the examples.

6. Customers can open an account with the stamp store by buying stamp cards issued by the post office so that they are guaranteed to have commemorative stamps issued during a given year.

7. In the two interactions between the clerk and her acquainted customers, the dialogue goes on until it is interrupted by another unacquainted customer. In this sense, there is no formal closing of the interaction.

8. The language reform campaign was started in the mid–1950s. The reform undertook two tasks. One was to promote a standard national language; the other was to simplify and standardize the writing system. In 1955 the name *Putonghua* (common language) was fixed to replace the name Mandarin for the standard national language.

9. It is a Chinese custom to send calendars to friends and relatives as a gift when the New Year is coming. Since the meeting took place toward the end of the year, it was understood that Lili was referring to this custom.

10. In China, urban families are better off than suburban and country residents.

11. Used throughout this study, the rank hierarchy refers to the ranking system for government officials. Since most of China's enterprises are state-run, employees in these enterprises or organizations are considered government employees whose incomes are determined by their rank in the system. Therefore, official rank not only gives a person social status, but also decides his/her economic status. Though the system is undergoing some changes due to China's economic reform started in 1979, it remains in substance the same.

12. Jianxin took part in some of the meetings that are used as data in chapter 4. During these meetings, he was quite active due to his relatively high rank position compared with other participants.

13. Studies on ellipsis and repetition as a device for solidarity and conversational involvement can be found in Tannen's (1989) work and Okazaki's (1994) study of ellipsis in Japanese.

References

Blom, J-P., & Gumperz, J. (1972). Social meaning in linguistic structure: Code-switching in Norway. In J. Gumperz & D. Hymes (Eds.), *Directions in sociolinguistics* (pp.407-34). Cambridge: Basil Blackwell.

Blum-Kulka, S. (1987). Indirectness and politeness in request: Same or different? *Journal of Pragmatics, 11,* 131–146.

Blum-Kulka, S. (1990). You don't touch lettuce with your fingers: Parental politeness in family discourse. *Journal of Pragmatics, 14,* 259–288.

Bond, M. H. (1994). *Beyond the Chinese face: Insights from psychology.* Oxford: Oxford University Press.

Brown, P., & Levinson, S. C. (1987). *Politeness: Some universals in language usage.* Cambridge: Cambridge University Press.

Cao, Y. Q. (1791). *Hong lou meng* [The dream of the red mansion]. Guangzhou: Hua-cheng Publishing House (Reprint).

Chang, H. C., & Holt, G. R. (1994). A Chinese perspective on face as inter-relational concern. In S. Ting-Toomey (Ed.), *The challenge of facework* (pp. 95–131). Albany: State University of New York.

Chao, Y. R. (1976). *Aspects of Chinese sociolinguistics.* CA: Stanford University Press.

Clark, H. H., & Schunk., D. H. (1980). Polite responses to polite requests. *Cognition, 8,* 111–143.

Coupland, J., Robinson, J. D., & Coupland, N. (1994). Frame negotiation in doctor-elderly patient consultations. *Discourse & Society, 5* (1), 89–124.

DeFrancis, J. (1984). *The Chinese language: Fact and fantasy.* Honolulu: University of Hawaii Press.

Ebrey, P. (1991). The Chinese family and the spread of Confucian values. In G. Rozman (Ed.), *The East Asian region: Confucian heritage and its modern adaption* (pp. 157–203). Princeton, NJ: Princeton University Press.

Erbaugh, M. S. (1995). Southern Chinese dialects as a medium for reconciliation within Greater China. *Language in Society, 24,* 79–94.

Ervin-Tripp, S. (1976). Is Sybil there? The structure of some American English directives. *Language in Society, 5,* 25–66.

Fang, H., & Heng, J.H. (1983). Social changes and changing address forms in China. *Language in Society, 12 (4)*, 495–509.

Fasold, R. (1990). *Sociolinguistics of language*. Cambridge: Basil Blackwell.

Fraser, B. (1981). On apologizing. In F. Coulmas (Ed.), *Conversational routine* (pp. 259–271). The Hague, The Netherlands: Mouton Publishers.

Giles, H. (1977). *Language, ethnicity and intergroup relations*. London: Academic Press.

Giles, H., Taylor, D. M., & Bourhis, R. (1973). Towards a theory of interpersonal accommodation through language: Some Canadian data. *Language in Society, 2*, 177–223.

Goffman, E. (1959). *The presentation of self in everyday life*. New York: Doubleday.

Goffman, E. (1967). *Interaction ritual: Essays on face to face behavior*. Garden City, NY: Doubleday.

Goffman, E. (1974). *Frame analysis*. New York: Harper & Row.

Goffman, E. (1981). *Forms of talk*. Philadelphia: University of Pennsylvania Press.

Grice, H. P. (1975). Logic and conversation. In P. Cole & J. L. Morgan (Eds.), *Pragmatics* (vol. 9, Syntax and semantics, pp. 113–128). New York: Academic Press.

Grimshaw, A. D. (Ed.). (1990). *Conflict talk*. Cambridge: Cambridge University Press.

Gu, Y. (1990). Politeness phenomena in modern China. *Journal of Pragmatics, 14* (2), 237–257.

Gu, Y. (1996a). Doctor-patient interaction as goal-directed discourse. *Journal of Asian Pacific Communication, 7* (3&4), 1–21.

Gu, Y. (1996b). *The changing modes of discourse in a changing China*. Plenary address, International Conference on Knowledge and Discourse, Beijing Foreign Studies University, Hong Kong.

Gu, Y., & Zhu, W. (1996). *Guan (Chinese officialdom) at work in discourse*. Unpublished manuscript, Beijing Foreign Studies University.

Gumperz, J.(1982). *Discourse strategies*. Cambridge: Cambridge University Press.

Harre, R., & Gillett, G. (1994). *The discursive mind*. Thousand Oaks, CA: Sage.

Heringer, J. T. (1977). Pre-sequences and indirect speech acts. In E. O. Keenan & T. Bennett (Eds.), *Discourse studies across time and space* (pp. 169–180). SCOPIL 5. University of Southern California, Linguistics Department.

Ho, D. Y. (1976). On the concept of face. *The American Journal of Sociology, 81*, 867–884.

Hsu, F. L. K. (1981). *American & Chinese: Passage to differences*. Honolulu: University of Hawaii Press.

Hu, H.C. (1944). The Chinese concept of "face." *American Anthropologist, 46*, 45–64.

Hwang, K.K. (1997). *Guanxi* and *Mientz*: Conflict resolution in Chinese society. *Intercultural Communication Studies, 7* (1), 17–42.

Hymes, D. (1962). The ethnography of speaking. In T. Gladwin and W.C. Sturtevant (Eds.), *Anthropology and human behavior* (pp. 13–53). Washington, DC: Anthropological Society of Washington.

Hymes, D. (1972). Models of the interaction of language and social life. In J.Gumperz & D. Hymes (Eds.), *Directions in sociolinguistics* (pp. 35–71). New York: Holt, Rinehart and Winston.

Hymes, D. (1974). *Foundations in sociolinguistics: An ethnographic approach*. Philadelphia: University of Pennsylvania Press.

Ide, S. (1982). Japanese sociolinguistics: Politeness and women's language. *Lingua, 57*, 357–387.

Ide, S. (1989). Formal forms and discernment: Two neglected aspects of universals of linguistic politeness. *Multilingual, 8* (2/3), 223–248.

King, A. (1992). *Zhongguo shehui yu wenhua.* [Chinese society and culture]. Hong Kong: Oxford University Press Ltd.

Kipnis, A. (1997). *Producing guanxi.* Durham, NC: Duke University Press.

Lakoff, R. (1973). The logic of politeness; or minding your p's and q's. Papers *from the ninth regional meeting of the Chicago Linguistic Society* (pp. 292–305). Chicago.

Lakoff, R. (1974). What you can do with words: Politeness, pragmatics and performatives. *Berkeley studies in syntax and semantics* (Vol. 1 (16), pp. 1–55). Institute of Human Learning, University of California, Berkeley.

Lakoff, R. (1979). Stylistic strategies within a grammar of style. *Language and Gender, 327,* 53–78.

Leech, G. N. (1983). *Principles of pragmatics.* London: Longmans.

Lehtonen, J.& Sajavaara, K. (1985). The silent Finn. In D. Tannen & M. Saville-Troike (Eds.), *Perspectives on silence.* Norwood, NJ: Ablex Publishing Corporation.

Lewis, R. (1996). *When cultures collide: Managing successfully across cultures.* London: Nicholas Brealey Publishing Limited.

Lii-Shih, Y. E. (1986). *Conversational politeness and foreign language teaching.* Taipei: Crane Publishing Co., Ltd.

Lii-Shih, Y. E. (1994). What do "yes" and "no" really mean in Chinese? In J. Alatis (Ed.), *Georgetown University round table on languages and linguistics.* Washington, DC: Georgetown University Press.

Liu, Z.F., and Lin, G. (1988). *Chuantong yu zhongguoren* [Tradition and Chinese]. Hong Kong: Joint Publishing Co., Ltd.

Luo, S.W. (1996). *Nuxing yu jindai zhongguo shehui* [Women and contemporary Chinese society]. Shanghai: People's Publishing House.

Mao, L. R. (1994). Beyond politeness theory: "Face" revisited and renewed. *Journal of Pragmatics, 21,* 451-486.

Manes, J. (1983). Compliments: A mirror of cultural values. In N. Wolfson & E. Judd (Eds.), *Sociolinguistics and language acquisition* (pp. 96–102). Cambridge: Newbury House Publishers, Inc.

Matsumoto, Y. (1988). Reexamination of the universality of face: Politeness phenomena in Japanese. *Journal of Pragmatics, 12,* 403–426.

Matsumoto, Y. (1989). Politeness and conversational universals—Observation from Japanese. *Multilingual, 8* (2/3), 207–221.

Merritt, M. (1976). On questions following questions in service encounters. *Language in Society, 5,* 315–357.

Merritt, M. (1984). On the use of "okay" in service encounters. In J. Baugh & J. Sherzer (Eds.), *Language in use* (pp. 139–147). Englewood Cliffs, NJ: Prentice-Hall.

Min, J. Y. (Ed.) (1995). *Yang gang yu yin ruo de bianzou: Liang xing guanxi he shehui moshi* [Changes in masculinity and femininity: The social model and relationship between the two sexes]. Beijing: Chinese Academy of Social Sciences.

Morisaki, S., & Gudykunst, W. B. (1994). Face in Japan and the United States. In S. Ting-Toomey (Ed.), *The challenge of facework* (pp. 47–93). Albany: State University of New York.

Nakane, C. (1970). *Japanese society.* Berkeley and Los Angeles: University of California Press.

Nakano, Y. (1995). *Frame analysis of a Japanese-American contract negotiation*. Unpublished doctoral dissertation, Georgetown University, Washington, DC.

Ng, S. H., & Bradac, J. J. (1993). *Power in language*. Newbury Park, CA: Sage.

Okazaki, S. (1994). *Ellipsis in Japanese conversational discourse*. Unpublished doctoral dissertation, Georgetown University, Washington, DC.

Olshtain, E., & Cohen, A.D. (1983). Apology: A speech-act set. In N. Wolfson & E. Judd (Eds.), *Sociolinguistics and language acquisition* (pp. 18–35). Cambridge: Newbury House Publishers.

Pan, Y. (1994). *Politeness strategies in Chinese verbal interaction: A sociolinguistic analysis of spoken data in official, business and family settings*. Unpublished doctoral dissertation, Georgetown University, Washington, DC.

Pan, Y. (1995). Power behind linguistic behavior: Analysis of politeness phenomena in Chinese official settings. *Journal of Language and Social Psychology, 14* (4), 462–481.

Pan, Y. (1996a). *Discourse patterns and politeness in the Chinese workplace*. Paper presented at Sociolinguistics Symposium 11, University of Wales, Cardiff, UK.

Pan, Y. (1996b). *Speaking for the other: Power recognition in Chinese official settings*. Paper presented at Georgetown Linguistics Society, Georgetown University, Washington, DC.

Pan, Y. (1997a). *Language use and conflicting identities: Chinese men and women at work and at home*. Paper presented at the 6th International Conference on Language and Social Psychology, Ottawa, Canada.

Pan, Y. (1997b). *You are my friend: Code-switching in Chinese service encounters*. Paper presented at the Annual Meeting of American Association of Applied Linguistics, Orlando, FL.

Pan, Y. (1999). Public literate design and ideological shift: A case study of Mainland China and Hong Kong. In J. Verschueren (Ed.), *Language and ideology: Selected papers from the 6th International Pragmatics Conference*, Vol. 1, 433-451. Antwerp: International Pragmatics Association.

Pan, Y. (in press a). Facework in Chinese service encounters. *Journal of Asian Pacific Communication*.

Pan, Y. (in press b). Code-switching and social changes in Hong Kong and Guangzhou service encounters. *International Journal of Society and Language*.

Pufahl, I. (1986). How to assign work in an office: A comparison of spoken and written directives in American English. *Journal of pragmatics, 10* (6).

Rodseth, L. (1998). Distributive models of culture. *American Anthropologist, 100* (1), 55–69.

Rozman, G. (Ed.). (1991). *The East Asian region*. Princeton, NJ: Princeton University Press.

Sajavaara, K. & Lehtonen, J. (1997). The silent Finn revisited. In A. Jaworski (Ed.), *Silence: Interdisciplinary perspective* (pp. 263–283). New York: Mouton de Gruyter.

Saville-Troike, M. (1989). *The ethnography of communication*. Cambridge: Basil Blackwell.

Schiffrin, D. (1984). Jewish argument as sociability. *Language in Society, 13,* 311–335.

Schiffrin, D. (1987). *Discourse markers*. Cambridge: Cambridge University Press.

Schiffrin, D. (1994). *Approaches to discourse*. Cambridge: Blackwell.

Scollon, R. (1998). *Mediated discourse as social interaction*. New York: Addison Wesley Longman Ltd.

Scollon, R., & Scollon, S.B.K. (1991). Topic confusion in English-Asian discourse. *World Englishes, 10* (2), 113–125.

Scollon, R., & Scollon, S.B.K. (1994). Face parameters in East-West discourse. In S. Ting-Toomey (Ed.), *The challenge of facework* (pp. 133–155). Albany: State University of New York Press.

Scollon, R., & Scollon, S.B.K. (1995). *Intercultural communication: A discourse approach.* Cambridge: Blackwell.

Scollon, S.B.K., & Pan, Y. (1997). *Generational and regional readings of the literate face in China.* Paper presented at China's Second Symposium on Intercultural Communication, Beijing, China.

Scollon, S.B.K., & Pan, Y. (forthcoming). *Saa Taaigik*: A metaphor for conflict avoidance. In D.C.S. Li (Ed.), *Discourse in search of members.* Stamford, CT: Ablex Publishing Corporation.

Scotton, C. M., & Zhu, W. (1983). *Tongzhi* in China: Language change and its conversational consequences. *Language in Society, 12* (4), 477–494.

Searle, J. R. (1976). A classification of illocutionary acts. *Language in Society, 5,* 1–23.

Shen, L. (Ed.). (1995). *A complete guide to Chinese laws.* Hong Kong: China Books Ltd (HK)

Shi, Z.W. (1997). *Jiating Wenhua: Hu! Hu! Hu!* [Family culture: Tiger! Tiger! Tiger!]. Beijing: China Industry and Commerce Joint Publishing House.

Shuy, R. (1982). Topic as the unit of analysis in a criminal law case. In D. Tannen (Ed.), *Analyzing discourse: Text and talk* (pp. 113–126). Washington, DC: Georgetown University Press.

Tannen, D. (1984). *Conversational style: Analyzing talk among friends.* Norwood, NJ: Ablex.

Tannen, D. (1986). *That's not what I meant!* New York: Ballantine.

Tannen, D. (1989). *Talking voices: Repetition, dialogue, and imagery in conversational discourse.* Cambridge: Cambridge University Press.

Tannen, D. (1990). *You just don't understand: Women and men in conversation.* New York: Ballantine.

Tannen, D. (1994). *Talking from 9 to 5.* New York: Avon Books.

Ting-Toomey, S. (1988). Intercultural conflict styles: A face-negotiation theory. In Y. Kim & W. Gudykunst (Eds.), *Theories in intercultural communication.* Newbury Park, CA: Sage.

Tracy, K. (1990). The many faces of facework. In H. Giles & W. P. Robinson (Eds.), *Handbook of language and social psychology.* Chichester, UK: John Wiley and Sons.

Trosborg, A. (1987). Apology strategies in natives/non-natives. *Journal of Pragmatics, 11,* 147–167.

Tu, W. M. (Ed.) (1994). *The living tree: The changing meaning of being Chinese today.* Stanford, CA: Stanford University Press.

Van Dijk, T. A. (Ed.) (1997). *Discourse as structure and process.* Thousand Oaks, CA: Sage.

Ventola, E. (1987). *The structure of social interaction: A systemic approach to the semiotics of service encounters.* London: Frances Pinter Publishers.

Vuchinich, S. (1990). The sequential organization of closing in verbal family conflict. In A. Grimshaw (Ed.), *Conflict talk* (pp. 118–138). Cambridge: Cambridge University Press.

Wierzbicka, A. (1991). *Cross-cultural pragmatics: The Semantics of Human Interaction.* Berlin: Mouton de Gruyter.

Wierzbicka, A. (1996). Constrastive sociolinguistics and the theory of "cultural scripts": Chinese vs. English. In M. Hellinger & U. Ammon (Eds.), *Contrastive sociolinguistics* (pp. 313–344). Berlin: Mouton de Gruyter.

Wolfson, N. (1983). An empirical based analysis of complimenting in American English. In N. Wolfson & E. Judd (Eds.), *Sociolinguistics and language acquisition* (pp. 82–95). Cambridge: Newbury House Publishers, Inc.

Wolfson, N., D'Amico-Reisner, L., & Huber, L. (1983). How to arrange for social commitments in American English: The invitation. In N. Wolfson & E. Judd (Eds.), *Sociolinguistics and language acquisition* (pp. 116–130). Cambridge: Newbury House Publishers, Inc.

Wu, W. (1995). Chinese evidence versus the institutionalized power of English. *Forensic Linguistics: The international journal of speech, language and the law, 2,* 2, 154–167.

Yamada, H. (1992). *American and Japanese business discourse: A comparison of interactional styles.* Norwood, NJ: Ablex Publishing.

Yamada, H. (1997). *Different games, different rules: Why American Japanese misunderstand each other.* New York and Oxford: Oxford University Press.

Yang, M. M. (1994). *Gifts, favors and banquets: The art of social relationships in China.* Ithaca, NY: Cornell University Press.

Young, L. W. L. (1982). Inscrutability revisited. In J. Gumperz (Ed.), *Language and social identity* (pp. 72–84). New York: Cambridge University Press.

Yu, X. (Ed.). (1989). *Jianming Zhongguo Baike Quanshu* [Concise encyclopedia of China]. Beijing: Chinese Academia of Social Sciences.

Yue, Q. (1989). *Jia guo jiegou yu zhongguoren* [The structure of family/country and Chinese people]. Hong Kong: China Publishing Co., Ltd.

Zhan, K. (1992). *The strategies of politeness in the Chinese language.* Berkeley, CA: Institute of East Asian Studies, University of California.

Zhang, Y. (1995). Indirectness in Chinese requesting. In G. Kasper (Ed.), *Pragmatics of Chinese as native and target language* (pp. 69–118). Honolulu, Hawaii: University of Hawaii, Second Language Teaching & Curriculum Center.

Zhao, G., & Gao, W. (Eds.). (1990). *Minzu yu wenhua* [Nationality and culture]. Nannin: Guangxi People's Publishing House.

Zheng, D. (1987). *Zhonghua minzu wenhua shi lun* [Introduction to the history of Chinese nationality and culture]. Hong Kong: Joint Publishing Co. (H.K.).

Zhu, W., & Chen, J. (1991). Some economic aspects of the language situation in China. *Journal of Asian Pacific communication, 2* (1), 91–111.

Author Index

W

Wierzbicka, A., 108, 109, 111, 150, *162*
Wolfson, N., 59, 151, *162*
Wu, W., 113, *162*

Y

Yamada, H., 68, 79, 150, *162*
Yang, M. M., 26, 27, 41, *162*
Young, L. W. L., *162*

Yu, X., 28, *162*
Yue, Q., 20, 106, 140, *162*

Z

Zhan, K., 17, *162*
Zhang, Y., 151, *162*
Zhao, G., 20, 40, 49, 78, 102, 147, *162*
Zheng, D., 20, *162*
Zhu, W., 54, 55, 79, *158, 162*

Subject Index

CPSIA information can be obtained
at www.ICGtesting.com
Printed in the USA
LVOW10s1134050118

561955LV00007B/46/P